Recovering from Chronic Fatigue Syndrome

Recovering from
Chronic Fatigue Syndrome

A Guide to Self-Empowerment

William Collinge, M.P.H., Ph.D.

THE BODY PRESS/PERIGEE

Grateful acknowledgment is given to Christine McNamara for illustrating this work, and to Charles Priest for designing the graphs.

The Body Press/Perigee Books
are published by
The Putnam Publishing Group
200 Madison Avenue
New York, NY 10016

Library of Congress Cataloging-in-Publication Data
Collinge, William
Recovering from chronic fatigue syndrome :
a guide to self-empowerment / by William Collinge.
        p.   cm.
    Includes index.
    ISBN 0-399-51807-X (acid-free paper)
    1. Chronic fatigue syndrome—Alternative treatment.
2. Mind and body therapies. I. Title.
RB150.F37C65   1993   92-35606 CIP
616′.047—dc20

Printed in the United States of America
1   2   3   4   5   6   7   8   9   10

This book is printed on acid-free paper.

Acknowledgments

I wish to express my appreciation to many people who contributed to this project: to Daniel Peterson, M.D., for his cooperation in helping establish the self-help training program in Incline Village, and his continuing support of this work; to Peter Madill, M.D., Jay Goldstein, M.D., Murray Susser, M.D., and Linda Miller Iger, Ph.D., for sharing their insights about clinical aspects of CFS; to Marya Grambs and The Chronic Fatigue Immune Dysfunction Syndrome Foundation, San Francisco, for permission to reproduce the treatment protocol from *CFIDS Treatment News;* and to Annabel Gregory for her logistical support.

I also thank Laura Yorke, my editor at Putnam, and her assistant, Eileen Cope, for their valuable help in preparing the manuscript; and Candice Fuhrman, my literary agent.

I am very grateful to the following teachers who have influenced my work a great deal: Leonard Duhl, M.D., and Henrik Blum, M.D., of the School of Public Health, Richard Lazarus, Ph.D., of the Department of Psychology, and Richard Barth, Ph.D., and Lonnie Snowden, Ph.D., of the School of Social Welfare, University of California, Berkeley; Lydia Temoshok, Ph.D., Langley Porter Institute, University of California, San Francisco (now with Walter Reed Army Hospital); and Jeru Kabbal of the A.P.T. Institute, San Rafael, California.

Finally, I thank the many patients who have allowed me to walk with them, and have shown me what it means to use illness as a teacher.

This book is dedicated to my daughter,
Rosalea Maia, who lets her light shine.

Contents

Foreword

In the fall of 1984, my quiet Internal Medicine practice was suddenly interrupted by the intrusion of a strange malady. Long-established, otherwise healthy patients developed a "flu-like" illness with low-grade fevers, swollen lymph nodes, headache, myalgias (muscle pains), and fatigue. Not so unusual, I thought, for a viral syndrome. Thus, I waited expectantly for everyone to recover.

The saga had, however, just begun. Many of the patients remained ill and, in fact, developed disabling fatigue, severe insomnia, intolerable myalgias, and even striking cognitive dysfunction such as inability to concentrate. Some became bedridden, losing jobs, financial resources, and even families.

Media attention to the phenomenon, spurred in part by the recent discovery of the AIDS virus, resulted in national and international attention to this disorder, which subsequently became labeled as Chronic Fatigue Immune Dysfunction Syndrome (CFIDS), more commonly known as Chronic Fatigue Syndrome (CFS). When some of the patients, approximately 20 percent, had not improved in the first two to three years of observation, it became clear that this is, indeed, a chronic and potentially disabling disease.

Now, several long years later, critical questions remain about the causation and exact disease process. Many researchers feel the course of this illness is most compatible with a prolonged viral infection. Others feel the primary abnormality is immune dysregulation (a disturbance in the regulation of immune system responses), in some cases leading to reactivation of latent viruses. Some physicians, at a loss to explain the myriad symptoms, resort to psychiatric diagnoses, such as conversion reactions or hypochondriasis.

Despite the mysteries accompanying this syndrome, its profound effects on victims and their families are clearly documented and definable. CFIDS is now recognized worldwide and across socioeconomic barriers. Any clinician who postpones treatment while wishfully waiting for complete definition of the disease totally ignores the plight of the suffering patient.

The argument that mind and body are separate, which has prevailed in medicine for many years, has slowed research into diseases affecting the whole person. This has produced disability and delayed therapy in many patients suffering from CFIDS and similar syndromes. Researchers must reach beyond this dichotomy and unite in the national scientific effort to better define the disease process. Potentially successful therapies can then be suggested for thousands of sufferers.

CFIDS physicians have sought and continue to seek the magic bullet of medicine that will lay this enemy forever to rest. Meanwhile, a number of therapies considered "band-aid" medicine have been found which afford some relief of symptoms. Examples include tricyclic antidepressants in low doses, certain axiolytics, and some immune modulating agents (e.g., gamma globulin). Based on the premise that CFIDS is due to immune dysregulation and viral reactivation, a few clinical trials are in progress with anti-viral and immune-regulating agents.

In the earlier years of this phenomenon, I gained much wisdom about CFIDS from listening to the patients. There were many whom I gradually began to see less frequently. These patients told me that they weren't "cured," but had come to a truce with their disease. They had modified their lifestyles or expectations and had learned to control or ameliorate their symptoms.

I then met William Collinge, who at the time was working with self-help programs for cancer and AIDS patients. While I was somewhat skeptical of mind/body medicine, largely due to my own lack of understanding and training, I referred many CFIDS patients to his program. The pilot program evolved into a structured approach for CFIDS patients and their significant others.

The results were striking. In short, many patients found themselves to be far more functional in their everyday living than they ever hoped possible. They gained a new understanding of their disease process. And their families, who experienced the real essence of the disease, could be trained to share true empathy and caring for the affected patient.

This experience has shown that CFIDS, like other chronic diseases, requires multi-disciplinary skills and expertise for successful management. Certainly patients require the help of basic scientists and compassionate, inquisitive primary care physicians. But they also need supportive services, including psychotherapy and self-help programs. Self-awareness, self-education, and self-help are critical to minimize the devastating effects of the illness and to achieve a functional, fulfilling life.

For clinicians, this book outlines an adjuvant therapy readily available to all CFIDS patients. The methods and philosophical approach espoused here represent critical steps toward our better understanding of the disease process and its treatment. Dr. Collinge summarizes an ever changing and ever broadening topic objectively, and bases his interventions on tried and true clinical experience.

Patients, please read and enjoy this book. With an open and receptive mind, the directives become clear. New understanding and healing may come very quickly. The profit will be yours at a low cost.

Daniel L. Peterson, M.D.
Incline Village, Nevada
Fall, 1992

Introduction

"I appreciate life more than I have ever appreciated it before. I believe that CFS has left me, although I understand that I'm still vulnerable, so when I get tired I get a little fear . . . I see life as a blessing now, and I don't take it for granted. I have more faith in myself, having made it through the worst year of my whole life.

"I thought about suicide. I didn't try it, but it was very attractive to me. Death would have been welcomed. I questioned how I was going to provide for myself.

"I believe I have more energy than before, but I'm more centered, more within myself and less concerned about my outer world. My energy has a different quality." —Linda

Perhaps you are reading these words because you or someone you know has Chronic Fatigue Syndrome (CFS), also known as Chronic Fatigue Immune Dysfunction Syndrome (CFIDS) or Myalgic Encephalomyelitis (ME). If this is the case, there is a fact you need to embrace right now, even though you may find it difficult to believe: *Recovery is possible.* I emphasize this at the outset because so often people with CFS lack belief in the possibility of healing. Rarely have they met a person like Linda, who can look *back* on CFS.

Why might the notion of recovery come as a surprise? It may be because of the syndrome's effects on one's morale and ability to envision a better future. Or it may be due to the social isolation that often comes with this syndrome. Perhaps it results from the media's sensational images of debilitation and hopelessness. Or it may be that a few support groups have inadvertently reinforced the image of "CFS victim." Or perhaps the syndrome simply has not been observed over a long enough period to shed much light on life after CFS.

This book is an outcome of the first complementary therapy program designed specifically for CFS. The term "complementary" refers to any approach that works alongside and supports established medical treatment. The program originated at Incline Village, Nevada, on the north shore of Lake Tahoe, as a result of the widely publicized outbreak of the mid 1980s. Our purpose was to help patients empower themselves to be full participants in their recovery.

With the cooperation of Daniel Peterson, M.D., co-discoverer of the outbreak, the program was based on a synthesis of research in behavioral medicine and CFS. This included insights gained from my work with exceptional cancer and AIDS patients—long-term survivors and those with unexpected recoveries. As with those other illnesses, profound lifestyle change, introspection, and self-help strategies are integral to recovery from CFS. There are of course features unique to this syndrome, and the program was tailored accordingly.

Our initial participants were referred by Dr. Peterson to complement his medical treatment. It soon became apparent that those who participated in this approach had better outcomes than those who relied on medical treatment alone. At this writing the program has served patients from fourteen states, and their family members. Patients have often cited this work as the turning point in their recovery.

In these pages you will learn the principles and strategies used by former CFS patients to heal physically, emotionally, and spiritually. You will hear in their own words what the healing process has been like for them. As a full, active participant in your treatment, you too will rediscover your health.

A note about labels: Another way of referring to a person with this syndrome is "PWC," for "Person with CFIDS." This term arose out of the need to affirm the authenticity of the syndrome, and to give patients a sense of shared identity. While I appreciate both of these concerns, I still prefer the less-than-perfect term "CFS patient" because it suggests the *transitory* nature of CFS, whereas "PWC" may inadvertently suggest an enduring identity. While I agree that calling oneself a PWC may be helpful, especially in the early stages of coping with the syndrome, my broader interest is in helping people *dis*-identify with the syndrome as a definition of who they are.

PART I

The Nature and Course of CFS

1

From Illness to Insight: Understanding CFS

"I went to over twenty doctors before I got the diagnosis of CFS. It was a tremendous relief. Even though there was no immediate cure, I finally knew what was wrong, and I had a name for it. I didn't think I was crazy, which had often been implied, but I was beginning to wonder."
　　　　　　　　　　　　　　　　　　　　　　　　　　—Delores

What Is CFS?

It is not uncommon for people to have seen over two dozen doctors before getting this diagnosis. While this problem is diminishing, it exists because CFS is the name for a syndrome, a "bag of symptoms," rather than for a cause. By contrast, strep throat, for example, is named for its known cause—the streptococcus bacterium—rather than its symptoms.

Because there is so much ambiguity surrounding this syndrome, many people with CFS have run a gauntlet of different diagnoses. Some of the most difficult to accept were those of depression or psychosomatic disorders, which seemed to blame the patient. Even worse for many was being given no diagnosis. In retrospect, these patients were treated most honestly, at least not having been mislabeled.

For anyone who has followed the research of the neurologic and immunologic abnormalities of this syndrome, there is no longer any question that it exists. However, there is naturally a period of lag time between when a new syndrome is identified and when the medical community at large integrates this new information. Fortunately the medical literature is acknowledging the existence of this syndrome and health-care providers are becoming informed about it. If your doctor seems uninformed or uninterested, you can get a list of recommended doctors in your area by contacting the organizations in Appendix D.

THE CHALLENGE OF MAKING THE DIAGNOSIS

Diagnosis of CFS is complicated by the fact that fatigue is the single most commonly reported complaint in physicians' offices. It is a feature of countless other conditions. Hence there is a need to rule out other illnesses, many of which have more concrete diagnostic criteria and well-defined treatments.

Figure 1 below helps put the problem of fatigue into perspective. The largest circle represents the general complaint of fatigue as a symptom for a wide range of conditions. The next smaller circle encompasses chronic fatigue—fatigue on a more enduring basis, but which could still be the result of a range of conditions. The smallest circle represents the distinct condition known as CFS or CFIDS, which includes a unique grouping of symptoms including brain and immune system irregularities. [1,2,3,4,5]

Figure 1. CFS in the broader context of fatigue complaints

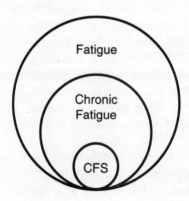

In 1988 the Centers for Disease Control (CDC) established certain tentative criteria for a diagnosis of CFS. The main points are:

(1) New onset of persistent or relapsing, debilitating fatigue or easy fatigability in a person who has no previous history of similar symptoms, that does not resolve with bed rest, and that is severe enough to reduce or impair average daily activity below 50 percent of the patient's premorbid (before illness) activity level for a period of at least six months.

(2) Other clinical conditions that may produce similar symptoms must be excluded by thorough evaluation, based on history, physical examination, and appropriate laboratory findings.[6]

These criteria were devised not as final guidelines for the diagnosis of CFS, but to help with identifying cases in the early study of the disease. As stated by the CFS Research Group at the CDC:
"[The] case definition was designed for purposes of conducting research and not for clinical diagnosis of CFS. This is an important distinction which is often misunderstood. . . . [It] is deliberately restrictive to ensure that most of the cases that meet it do in fact have CFS. Although many true CFS patients may be excluded by this definition, a less restrictive definition would also include a number of non-CFS patients."[7]

It is not the purpose of this book to focus on the nuances of diagnosis or medical treatment. These should be addressed through direct consultation with competent medical help. The interested reader is referred to Appendix A for more detail about the CDC diagnostic criteria, and Appendix B for a summary of known medical treatments. It is my purpose to offer a practical, realistic perspective on the syndrome once diagnosed, and on how to fully participate in your recovery. Toward this end, let us consider what CFS really is.

A DEFINITION

There have been countless attempts to characterize this syndrome, usually with long, cumbersome lists of symptoms, but great progress has been made in refining our understanding. One of the most concise descriptions is offered by Jay Goldstein, M.D., Director of the Chronic Fatigue Institute in Beverly Hills, California, who states:

"There is an increasing consensus that CFS is a virally induced, cytokine-mediated psychoneuroimmunologic disorder that occurs in genetically predisposed individuals."[8]

This brief yet thorough definition is tremendously significant. If you can understand each of its parts, you will understand much about not only CFS, but the predominant health crises of this decade including cancer, environmental illness, AIDS, and even heart disease. Before we examine the parts of this explanation more closely, let us first step back to view it in a broader context.

The Multicausal Perspective

The significance of Goldstein's statement is that it embodies the "multicausal perspective." This represents a historic shift in how the medical world thinks about what determines health and illness.[9] The shift is from a single-cause approach to a multicausal approach.

In the multicausal perspective, health status is the outcome of several factors working together, not a single factor such as a virus. These factors include heredity, environment, lifestyle, and medical treatment (see illustration below). They operate together to determine your resistance to illness, as well as the timing and severity of illness. Let us look more closely at each of these factors before we return to the description of CFS.

Figure 2. The multicausal perspective on health

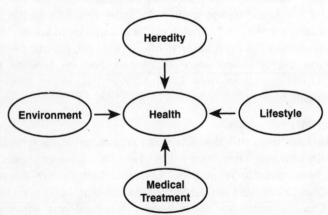

HEREDITY

We take for granted that our height and hair color are genetically determined, yet there are also genetic differences in how our immune systems function. This makes one person more vulnerable to certain types of cancer, another to certain types of viruses, and leaves a third perhaps more vulnerable to autoimmune diseases like multiple sclerosis or rheumatoid arthritis. A fourth person may be effectively resistant to all these immune-related diseases, yet may succumb to a disease process in another system, such as heart disease. This helps explain how a genetically determined vulnerability may be a factor in CFS.

ENVIRONMENT

Obviously pathogens such as viruses and bacteria come from the environment around you. But the influence of the environment on your health also includes toxins and pollutants that have accumulated in your body and may affect your resistance to illness. For example, growing up downwind from a nuclear testing site in the 1950s or in a farming community where agricultural chemicals had seeped into the water table, can have a definite impact on your resistance. And of course there are the petrochemicals and other substances in your current environment, some of which we have yet to discover, which may chronically disturb your immune functioning.

MEDICAL TREATMENT

Various kinds of medical treatment that you have received over your lifetime can support your immune system while others may actually weaken it. For instance, there is evidence that antibiotics, though having saved countless lives, may actually weaken immunity under some circumstances. This is especially true in people who have had many courses of antibiotics or taken them for a long period of time. The effects may be direct, via the chemicals affecting white cell functioning. Or they may be indirect, by altering the intestinal flora in a way that fosters yeast overgrowth, with the toxic by-products of yeast activity weakening immunity.

Also there is an interesting debate over whether immunizations may interfere with normal immunity. Most of us growing up in the second half of this century have had heavy doses of antibiotics and various immunizations. Many other drugs we commonly take have not been around long enough to truly reveal their long-term effects.

LIFESTYLE

Lifestyle includes your patterns of rest and exercise, work and play habits, nutrition, loving relationships, emotional stress, self-help practices, and your attitudes toward living. All these factors have impact on the body's ability to resist illness. In the case of an illness such as CFS where there is no proven medical cure, this aspect of the multicausal perspective takes on even greater significance.

While there's not much you can do about your heredity, your past environment or past medical treatments, you can live a health-promoting lifestyle now. For example, you can avoid the standard American diet (known as "the S.A.D.")—high fat, high sugar, low fiber, processed foods—to eat a healthy, whole-foods diet. You can alter your habits of work, play, and how you relate to others to reduce stress and have a greater balance of relaxation and exercise. And you can become an active participant in your health through self-empowerment strategies (which we will discuss in a later chapter). Lifestyle is the area over which you have the greatest control on a daily basis in recovering from CFS.

Lifestyle is also of great interest because of findings in the field of psychoneuroimmunology (PNI). This area of research explains how the brain and immune system communicate with each other, via the nervous system and chemical messengers in the blood. The relevance of this for lifestyle is that the mental, emotional, and spiritual aspects of your life can have impact, both positively and negatively, on your immune functioning.

However, while PNI helps us see how the mind can help or harm our immune responses, it also shows us why recovery from CFS is not simply a question of "mind over matter." With this illness, matter—or the disease process in the physical body—affects mind as well. As we shall see later, the symptoms of CFS, including such cognitive problems as memory loss, anxiety, depression, and difficulty concentrating, are probably caused by the chemical by-products of the disease process.

Putting It All Together

With this background, let us now consider the evidence for each part of Goldstein's description of CFS.

"VIRALLY INDUCED"

A virus is an environmental input which may serve as a trigger for the syndrome. It is not yet known whether we are dealing with a single virus or more than one. For a time it was thought that human herpesvirus number 6 (HHV6), discovered in 1987, might be the culprit. HHV6 infiltrates the T and B cells of the immune system, compromising their ability to protect the body from other viral infections. It also attacks certain neurological and intestinal tissue, and so is implicated in a great deal of the symptomatology. [10,11]

Recent thinking, however, is that HHV6 is probably not acting alone in CFS. More likely, this very common virus is reactivated from its normally latent state by immunologic dysfunction that is caused by yet another agent, possibly another virus. The theory is that this, along with other latent viruses such as Epstein Barr and Cytomegalovirus, become active and create their typical symptoms because the immune system has become unable to keep them in their normal latent state.

This theory is supported by one of the most comprehensive studies of CFS, which was published in the prestigious journal *Annals of Internal Medicine* in January 1992.[12] It was based on a study of 259 patients from the practice of Daniel Peterson, M.D., and his then-partner Paul Cheney, M.D., in Incline Village, Nevada in the mid 1980s (hereafter called "the Tahoe study"). Two-thirds of the patients were female, the average age was 38 + years, around 40 percent were college graduates, and the median length of illness at the time had reached 1.3 years.

This study, the largest of its kind, compared these patients with a healthy control group. It gives us one of the clearest pictures yet of the neurologic and immunologic aspects of CFS. Some of the findings included:

1. A significantly elevated T-cell ratio (3.16 versus 2.3 for the healthy comparison group). This is the ratio of T-helper to

T-suppressor cells in the immune system. These cells and their ratios will be discussed more in Chapter 4, but this finding indicates that the immune system is trying hard to respond to something.

2. Significantly more activity of the HHV6 virus. Active replication of the virus was found in 79 percent of the patients, and only 20 percent of the controls.

3. Lesions in the brain tissue, as revealed by magnetic resonance imaging (MRI), were found in 78 percent of patients compared to 21 percent of the controls.

The strong implication is that the patients were experiencing a chronic, immunologically-mediated inflammatory process of the central nervous system. The heightened activity of HHV6, ordinarily a latent herpesvirus in healthy people, may explain a great deal of the symptoms of CFS. HHV6 inhabits certain cells of the immune and nervous systems, as well as the intestinal tract.

A Retrovirus Connection?

Researchers working independently on both coasts have recently discovered evidence of a new virus which shows strong evidence as a possible trigger for CFS. It is a previously unknown member of the class of viruses known as "retroviruses." A retrovirus is a type of virus that attaches itself to a cell wall, then it penetrates the cell. Once inside, it sheds its outer coat. Then the RNA (genetic material) that was inside the retrovirus turns itself into DNA (another form of genetic material), and incorporates itself into the genetic material—the chromosome—of the human cell. In other words, the retrovirus infiltrates the genetic material of the human cell and commandeers its machinery, using it to make copies of the retrovirus RNA. These copies go out of the cell and become separate retroviral particles that can infect other cells.

In 1990 a team of researchers at the Wistar Institute in Philadelphia discovered evidence of a retrovirus in 80 percent of a sample of thirty CFS patients, both adults and children. Similar evidence of exposure was present in a third of twenty healthy people exposed to the patients. However, *no* evidence of the retrovirus was found in twenty healthy, unrelated people.

These findings suggest the possibility that a retrovirus may be involved in causation of CFS. If this is the case, it may act by integrating itself into the genetic material of immune cells and then alter immune functioning, thereby causing dysregulation or chronic activation of immune responses. [13,14]

At the University of Southern California, John Martin, M.D., Ph.D., a prominent CFS researcher, has cultured a retrovirus from the blood and cerebrospinal fluid of several CFS patients. The particular virus he isolated is called a "foamy" virus, and belongs to a subclass of retroviruses called "spumaviruses." This type of virus has been largely unknown or unrecognized in humans, but has been known to infect animals. Interestingly, many animals carry this type of virus yet remain perfectly healthy. Dr. Martin believes this spumavirus may be a trigger for CFS by disturbing immune cell functioning. [15,16]

According to Dr. Elaine DeFreitas of the Wistar Institute research team, the theory of a retrovirus as a causal factor is complicated by the fact that retroviruses are thought to be transmitted only by vital bodily fluids, and the risky behavior necessary for this does not fit the typical CFS patient. If this retrovirus is the long-sought trigger, understanding how it is transmitted will be a crucial question. [17]

"Cytokine-Mediated"

Cytokines are special hormones which the immune cells produce in their attempts to protect the body from infection. Symptoms of CFS may result from a chronic overproduction of cytokines. In effect, the immune system is stuck in the "full on" position, and its ability to "down-regulate" is impaired. Tremendously high levels of certain cytokines—specifically interleukin II (IL2) and interferon—have been found in CFS patients. These substances are used in cancer therapy to fight tumors, and as a side effect, routinely produce the symptoms of CFS in cancer patients. Of course the symptoms abate when treatment is ended. [18]

"Psychoneuroimmunologic Disorder"

Mind, brain, nervous system, and immune system all affect, and are affected by, this disease process. It follows that the flow of communication among these systems may also be altered. In fact, many authorities assert that the involvement of CFS in the brain tissue and cognitive functioning are the most important and debilitating features of the syndrome.[19] We will discuss these symptoms in greater detail in Chapter 2.

"Genetically Predisposed Individuals"

Some of us are more vulnerable than others to this condition, based on hereditary differences in how our immune systems respond to the viruses or other pathogens involved.

One of the most important insights about genetic influences is offered by AIDS research. HIV, a retrovirus, is the most studied virus in history, and more is known about the immune response in AIDS than in any other viral illness. A research team led by Mary Claire King at the University of California, Berkeley, recently discovered a genetic pattern in people with HIV that may account for *reduced* susceptibility to AIDS. As a result of these findings, a great deal of the tremendous individual variation in how the disease progresses can be explained.[20] Most likely this applies to other viral diseases too, and it is consistent with theories of CFS which include a genetic predisposition to the syndrome.

In summary, CFS affects the whole person. It is not a simple communicable disease, attributable to a single cause. Rather it is a result of multiple factors coming together. According to Dr. Seymour Grufferman, Chairman of Epidemiology and Preventive Medicine at the University of Pittsburgh, "It is likely that chronic fatigue syndrome has many etiologies and is a common outcome of several pathogenic pathways .... The occurrence of a disease in clusters suggests that infectious agents or other common source environmental agents play a role in the etiology of the disease."[21]

CFS as an Opportunistic Illness

When we consider the multiple influences on our health, it is clear that there are many factors which affect our resistance. And when a state of compromise or weakened resistance is present, this makes it easier for a pathogen, such as a virus, to gain a foothold and trigger a disease process. An illness that arises out of such a state of vulnerability is called an "opportunistic" illness.

Perhaps the simplest example of an opportunistic illness is the common cold. We have all had experiences where we developed a cold after some specific stressful experience, such as travel to another climate, a period of emotional upset, final exams, or racing for a deadline. While cold viruses are constantly around us, it is only under certain circumstances that they find the opportunity to get a foothold.

The notion of opportunistic illness applies to other illnesses too. For instance, it is well known that all of us have cancer cells in our bodies, but few of us develop cancer. Most adults carry the Epstein-Barr virus (the cause of mononucleosis), but not all have had mononucleosis. And studies indicate that not everyone who is HIV-positive develops AIDS. In fact, a few have even converted back to HIV-negative. [22,23]

Research with CFS strongly indicates that this too is an opportunistic illness. The presence of its causal agent(s) is *necessary but not sufficient* to cause CFS. That is, not everyone who is exposed to the agent(s) develops CFS. This is evidenced by the fact that few spouses of people with CFS, presumably having also been exposed, develop the condition. At this time we do not know whether there are any particular factors that might predispose someone to developing CFS.

If and when a specific viral trigger for CFS is confirmed, it is likely that it will also be found in other people who do not develop the disease. In keeping with the principle of multicausality, it too will probably be considered necessary but not sufficient for the illness.

Host Resistance

In order for pathogens such as viruses to flourish, they need a receptive *host*. This means a person whose resistance to those pathogens has already been compromised. And when these pathogens do not flourish, it is because host resistance has successfully kept them in check. In the case of CFS, the immune system is at the heart of host resistance.

The concept of host resistance was the bone of contention in the celebrated struggle between two famous French researchers during the nineteenth century. Claude Bernard asserted that the "terrain," or the environment within the individual, is what allows disease to develop, and should receive the highest priority in research. For example, if you take a worm out of the moist earth and isolate it on a rock in the sun, it will die. The worm requires a very specific terrain in order to flourish.

Louis Pasteur, Bernard's contemporary, argued vehemently that the presence of individual pathogens—germs—was more important in determining health, and they should be the focus of research. This bitter rivalry continued for years. However, on his deathbed, Pasteur recanted and made his famous statement that "The pathogen is nothing, the terrain is everything."

However, because CFS is an opportunistic illness relying on weakened host resistance, and because host resistance is very much affected by the behavior of the individual, there is a lot you can do to influence the course of your illness. Self-help and lifestyle change are means by which you can alter the terrain within your body to promote healing.

Recovery: What Does It Mean?

With regard to CFS, "recovery" is a highly charged term that means different things to different people. The complex nature of this syndrome provokes us to look carefully at our use of this word. With many other illnesses, recovery usually suggests a "return to the old," recovering the old way of life, resuming the activities and lifestyle to which we had grown accustomed. Yet, one of the greatest mistakes people with CFS can make is to hold a vision of recovery as "returning to the way I was living before I got sick." The difficulty is that, given the multicausal perspective, the way you were living before you got sick may have been a co-factor in your getting sick.

This raises the question of what it *is* that we hope to recover. Obviously, if you believe that certain lifestyle factors may have contributed to your vulnerability to CFS, and your vision is to return to those same conditions, then in that sense recovery is not likely to endure (and is presumably undesirable). If, on the other hand, recovery means re-establishing a sense of equilibrium, control, harmony, and quality in your life, then yes, recovery is desirable and possible.

Below we will explore these two broad perspectives on the meaning of recovery. One looks at recovery in quantitative terms, the other in qualitative terms.

QUANTITATIVE RECOVERY:
A PRIOR LEVEL OF FUNCTIONING

Many clinicians and people with CFS think of recovery in terms of activity level or level of daily functioning. This entails a comparison of your current activity level and energy level to your pre-illness levels. This of course is the first concern most people have, since it addresses the most obvious source of distress with CFS—not being able to do things in daily functioning like we did before. In this view, full recovery means a full return to pre-illness levels.

Clinical experience indicates that in terms of activity level many patients improve in two to four years, though not necessarily back to pre-illness levels. There is, however, a range of responses. There are those who seem to improve faster. I have known former patients who, through learning the art of moderation, have been able to run, Windsurf, or ski again. On the other hand, as observed by Jay Goldstein, M.D., of the Chronic Fatigue Syndrome Institute of Beverly Hills, there are a minority of patients who experience progressive worsening of symptoms.[24]

While it is impossible to predict for a given individual what degree of activity will be reclaimed, there is plenty of reason for hope of re-establishing a satisfactory level of functioning. This is especially true for those who take an active role in health promotion. What is "satisfactory" is of course a subjective judgment, and depends a great deal on your expectations and standards for what is acceptable.

QUALITATIVE RECOVERY:
A SENSE OF EQUILIBRIUM AND CONTROL

I have known many former patients who describe themselves as recovered from CFS, but whose outward lives look very different from before the illness. From the quantitative point of view, they might be working fewer hours, getting less achieved, exercising with less intensity or duration, taking more rest than before, and paying more attention to managing their energy. Yet there has been a dramatic positive change in their sense of equilibrium and control in their lives. There is a new understanding and respect for the body's responses to stress or challenge.

Their values and interests have changed, making them more appreciative of what they have. They may place less emphasis on outward performance or achievement, and more emphasis on living in harmony with their relationships and their surroundings. And amid all these changes has arisen a clearer sense of purpose, meaning, and living in balance, qualities that they did not have before the illness.

As a result, the recovery they are describing is not a matter of picking up where they left off. Rather it is a departure from the direction they had been taking before, an expansion into new ways of living that make their lives richer and more meaningful. For many, this "recovery" has taken place while adjusting to and accepting a level of overall energy and outward functioning that is lower than what they had prior to CFS.

We will explore the meaning of recovery at greater length in the next chapter. For now, consider the proposition that where CFS is concerned, *re*covery and *dis*covery go hand in hand. The goal should not be limited to recovering the old, in the quantitative sense; it should include discovering the new. For some it takes courage to accept that this illness may signal the end of one way of life and the beginning of another. For others, this may come as a relief.

Recovery from CFS is both a challenge and an adventure, and as you will see later in the stories of others, unexpected rewards await you.

2

Onset and the Chronic Phase: Symptoms and Cycles

"It was like I was in a coma. You could have driven a truck through my room and I wouldn't have awakened." —Sarah

"I would lie there for hours, totally exhausted, but unable to sleep." —Debbie

These statements are an example of the extremes this syndrome encompasses. Few diseases have as diverse an array of symptoms. There have been many attempts to describe the symptom picture in CFS, and the subject is complicated by the fact that there are such tremendous differences among individuals with the syndrome.

For example, while the fatigue is present in virtually all cases, in some people it is not necessarily the most debilitating symptom at a given point in time during the course of the illness. At times they may experience a great deal more distress because of the cognitive disturbance. For someone else, the muscle aches and painful lymph nodes may be the most troubling symptoms. Still, most people experience all the symptoms at some point. It is the severity, chronicity, and patterns of the symptoms that set this syndrome apart from many other illnesses. In this chapter we will describe the onset, survey the major symptoms, and describe the cyclical nature of CFS.

Onset

The Tahoe study found that about 87 percent of patients' chronic fatigue started suddenly accompanied by flu, cold, or apparent viral infection (the latter characterized by at least two of the following: fever, headache, myalgias, sore throat, earache, congestion, runny nose, cough, diarrhea, and fatigue).

While onset is generally acute with the above symptoms, in a few cases it has begun with another illness, or some other stressor such as pregnancy. There are many theories about how onset is triggered, but the end result seems to be that the immune system becomes stuck in a state of hyper-activation. This involves the chronic over-production of chemicals (cytokines) which ordinarily help activate a healthy immune response. When overproduced to such an extreme, they become toxic to the body and cause the symptoms of CFS.

Symptoms

COGNITIVE DYSFUNCTION

There is a growing consensus among researchers that cognitive dysfunction, or disturbance in mental functioning, is a must for a diagnosis of CFS. In fact, Paul Cheney, M.D., describes this as "a disease of cognitive dysfunction." And according to Byron Hyde, M.D., Chair of the Nightingale Research Foundation, brain dysfunction is a requirement in defining the syndrome. The area of the brain affected varies from one person to the next, although almost all are found to have injury to the left frontal lobe. Damage to this area of the brain is responsible for several of the disturbances of memory, concentration, and other cognitive symptoms of CFS.[1] The Tahoe study found 78 percent of the patients to have lesions in their brain tissue, as revealed by magnetic resonance imaging, and this would certainly help explain the list of cognitive symptoms below. There are many cognitive impairments that are common, including:

problems with memory sequencing
spatial disorganization

trouble giving and following directions
difficulty processing problems
slow intellectual speed
difficulty processing visual and auditory information
forgetfulness
irritability
mental confusion
inability to concentrate
impairment of speech and/or reasoning
light-headedness, or feeling in a fog
word-finding problems
distractibility
difficulty processing more than one thing at a time
inability to perform simple math functions
problems with verbal recall
motor problems
disturbance in abstract reasoning
sequencing problems
memory consolidation (extracting information from the environ-
    ment and laying it down in the form of a memory)
short-term memories being easily distorted or perturbed

The most common cognitive symptom is difficulty concentrating, found in over 80 percent in the Tahoe study. Many patients consider the cognitive symptoms the most devastating, more than even the fatigue, pain, or the inability to work. The situation is made worse by the fact that to cope with or adjust to the debilitation of the illness requires mental and emotional resources. With these disturbed, the sense of helplessness and frustration can be compounded.

SLEEP DISTURBANCE
Sixty-three percent of patients in the Tahoe study were found to have sleep difficulties. Problems can be either of interrupted sleep or inability to remain awake. And when sleep is managed, it is not refreshing sleep. Rather, one awakens still feeling exhausted, or may feel exhausted after just a few minutes out of bed.

This is perhaps the most important symptom to treat in CFS. Good quality rest is necessary in order for the body's self-repair mechanisms to work effectively, and it takes time for the immune system to heal itself. Yet because of the chronic immune activation, the immune system is churning out substances around the clock which disturb the sleep center of the brain. In addition, many people with CFS have chills or night sweats which add to the difficulty. The sleep disturbance is aggravated by anxiety about the consequences of not being able to sleep.

EMOTIONAL DISTURBANCE

Seventy percent of the patients in the Tahoe study were found to have problems with anxiety, depression, or mood changes. There is a wide range of emotional problems that may accompany CFS, as is the case with many other chronic illnesses. However, CFS is different from many other conditions in that the activity of the disease process itself affects brain chemistry, neurological functioning, and emotions directly.

In this sense, much of the emotional difficulty could be called somato-psychic—that is, resulting from problems in the soma, or body, affecting the mind or psyche. In the words of Mark Demitrack, M.D., Senior Collaborating Scientist, Clinical Neuroendocrinology Branch, National Institute of Mental Health, "Psychiatric symptoms reflect . . . the direct involvement of the brain and central nervous system in the overall pathophysiology of this illness."[2]

Remember, our emotional experiences can be triggered by events in either the mind or the body, and there is usually an interaction between the two. Originating in the mind, our emotions can cause changes in the body. And events in the body can change our chemistry and affect our thoughts.

Because this fact is poorly understood by many health professionals, and especially mental health professionals, CFS patients often end up believing that their emotional disturbances are entirely the result of flaws in their attitudes or in their understanding of how to cope with life.

Of course the simple fact of living with a chronic illness and all the uncertainty it brings is also cause for emotional stress. It is impossible to determine how much emotional disturbance is the direct result of the disease process and how much is a result of the psychological stress of having the illness. Yet many patients breathe a sigh of relief when they realize that they are not crazy and that their emotional disturbance is most likely attributable to the activity of the disease process.

Of the emotional symptoms, most prominent are anxiety and depression. Also common are panic attacks, mood swings, and personality changes. All these problems are frequently accompanied by catastrophic fantasies about what the future holds, which can accelerate or deepen the distress. Another common occurrence which tends to exacerbate these symptoms is shortness of breath.

It is not uncommon for people with CFS, especially with the more severe cases, to have suicidal thoughts or feelings. This is entirely understandable and nothing to be ashamed of. In a sense, it represents the inner child's desperate wish to escape from a seemingly impossible situation.

FATIGUE

In the Tahoe study, about 6 percent were bedridden, about 28 percent could only work part-time, and less than half could fulfill all their home or work activities (with no energy left for anything else).

The fatigue that comes with CFS is usually an overwhelming, debilitating kind much more severe than that arising from normal exertion. Sometimes it is experienced in waves, accompanied by nausea. There may be a pattern where certain times of the day it is less severe. There is a wide range of severity, and some people must remain in bed eighteen or more hours per day, barely able to drag themselves to the bathroom. Others are able to function in a job relatively normally until "hitting a wall" of fatigue at the same time each afternoon.

For many, this is the most distressing symptom of the syndrome. While they may have a pattern or cycle of relatively good days followed by periods of severe depletion, their "good days" are never as good as before they became ill.

Another aspect of the fatigue is called "post exertional malaise." Many people with CFS are able to exercise moderately and feel fine while doing it. However, a few hours later or the next day they may find themselves with a major flare-up of symptoms.

CARDIAC SYMPTOMS

Heart irregularities are reported by approximately 40 percent of people with CFS.[3] The most common symptoms are chest pain, shortness of breath, arrhythmia, missed heartbeats, rapid heartbeats, and chest pounding.[4] Fortunately, the consensus among CFS experts is that the cardiac symptoms do not represent serious coronary problems. They may represent problems absorbing magnesium, an element widely used to remedy such symptoms; muscular weakness in the diaphragm; fibromyalgia, muscle aches and pains which are a common feature of CFS; or myocarditis, infection in the tissues surrounding the heart. Of course, other forms of heart disease are possible independent of the syndrome and should be ruled out.

SENSORY DYSFUNCTION

The senses are also affected, which is not surprising with a syndrome affecting the person on such a global scale. Sensitivity may be dramatically increased to cold and heat, sound, light, and touch. Between 40 and 68 percent in the Tahoe study were found to have odd sensation in the skin. There may at times be numbness in the face or extremities, burning in the hands or feet, or problems with dizziness and balance.

Disturbances of vision are quite common and include blurred vision, sensitivity to light (called "photophobia"), eye pain, frequent prescription changes, seeing spots, a variety of neuromuscular dysfunctions in the eyes.

PAIN

There are a variety of types of pain associated with CFS. They include headaches, pain in the joints, painful lymph nodes, back pains, chest pains, and rashes. Muscle pain can be similar to that which most of us have experienced when we have had the flu, except it is on a chronic basis. This is a generalized, dull aching in the muscles and joints. There may also be sharp pains in specific muscle groups. The terms "myalgia" and "arthralgia" are often used to describe chronic muscles pains, aching, and tenderness of this sort. In the Tahoe study about 85 percent were found to have myalgias and headaches, and about 75 percent had swollen lymph glands.

It is now thought that the disease known as "fibromyalgia" may actually be related to CFS, and that the two may be expressions of the same disease process. Fibromyalgia has also been a disease in search of a specific cause, possibly viral. It is characterized by chronic musculoskeletal pain, tender points, and fatigue, and has many other symptoms of CFS. It is the second or third most common diagnosis in the field of adult rheumatology, with a prevalence rate estimated at around three to six million patients in the U.S.[5] The more we learn about fibromyalgia and CFS, the less we are able to distinguish them as separate entities. Increasingly, fibromyalgia is being included among the diagnostic criteria for CFS.

GASTROINTESTINAL DISTURBANCES AND WEIGHT CHANGES

Gastrointestinal disturbances include new onset of food allergies and sensitivities, vomiting, yeast overgrowth in the gut, abdominal pain, constipation, irritable bowel, intolerance to alcohol, and bloating. Many patients are diagnosed as having irritable bowel syndrome. In the Tahoe study over 35 percent were found to have problems with diarrhea, 47 percent with stomach aches, over half with nausea, and 38 percent with loss of appetite.

Another common occurrence is weight change, either up or down. About 27 percent had gains of at least ten pounds, while about 14 percent had losses of at least ten pounds.

SORE THROAT, COUGH, AND FEVER

The Tahoe study found over three quarters of patients to have problems with recurrent sore throat, 53 percent with cough, and over 46 percent with recurrent fevers at home.

OTHER SYMPTOMS

There is a mixture of other symptoms associated with the syndrome for many people, including intermittent swelling of the fingers, eczema, other rash, hair loss, low body temperature, menstrual problems, and endometriosis.

What Course Do the Symptoms Take?

It is reassuring to know that unlike other chronic illnesses, CFS typically does not have a "progressive downhill course" of getting worse over time. Rather, it is characterized by an acute onset followed by a chronic phase with cyclical waxing and waning of symptoms. The cycles gradually diminish in intensity as you move into the recovery phase (the subject of the next chapter).

CFS has, however, a wide range of symptom severity. This is unlike other viral illnesses with a much narrower variation in severity, as, for example, in the common cold, mononucleosis, or chicken pox.

We can understand these extreme individual differences from the insights of the AIDS research mentioned in Chapter 1. There are genetically determined differences in how people's bodies respond to a disease process.

THE CHRONIC PHASE

The chronic phase is marked by settling into cycles of symptom severity. The degree of disability might vary according to a pattern for the individual. For many, the cyclical nature of CFS makes the road to recovery a bumpy one. In a few people, especially in more severe cases, there may not be such obvious cycles, but a more steady unrelenting state of debilitation.

Figure 3. An example of how the level of functioning can vary from onset through the chronic phase

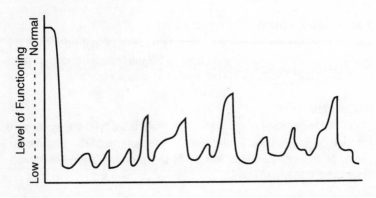

It is a common occurrence for a person to go into a period of remission—the reduction of symptoms—and feel so excited about it that they try to make up for all the lost time and activity very quickly. This of course can bring on a relapse—the return of symptoms—shortly afterward. We will discuss this problem and how to prevent it in Chapter 5.

Remissions can be great or slight, brief or long. They may follow a regular pattern or an irregular pattern. Some symptoms may go into remission while certain others remain. One of my patients, Helen, had a pattern in which her fatigue symptoms would improve markedly, but her mental confusion might not improve to such a noticeable degree. With a little self-examination, you should be able to describe the pattern your remissions take.

Many relapses are triggered by stressful events, which can be either physical or emotional. This can include positive experiences such as a family wedding, a vacation, or a holiday period, as well as negative events like marital problems, a car accident, or financial worries. No doubt you have been able to point to particular stresses as triggering a relapse.

However, some relapses occur simply because of the cyclical nature of the disease process in CFS and cannot be attributed to particular stresses. You can be living a relatively stress-free life and doing all the right things, and you will still have relapses.

In the chronic phase, one of the biggest dangers to avoid is the tendency to resign yourself to being a "helpless victim" with an "incurable" illness. You can learn to monitor your patterns of remission and relapse. You can soften the impact of the relapses by anticipating them and taking action to support your body with extra rest or other forms of self-care. And you can arm yourself with the knowledge that recovery is possible. In the next chapter we will explore the transition into the recovery phase.

3

The Recovery Phase: When and Why Recovery Happens

"My road to recovery has been bumpy. Many times I've gone two steps forward and one step back. There was a lot of fear when I started feeling really good, because I thought 'It's not going to last,' or 'Gee, I'm feeling well, this isn't right.' My self-image was still that 'I'm sick.' It took a long time to accept feeling good without fear of relapse.

"I consider myself recovered. But I'm not back where I was, I'm many steps further, because I'm a different person now. To go back to where I was would mean going backwards. I've grown and learned so much about myself that there's no way that I would want to go back. All of my attitudes and perceptions were out of whack, and I really needed to look into them.

"I'm in a whole different place in my life. I feel I can do everything I want to do, that my life is happier than it has ever been. I have a better idea of who I am, and I am more at peace." —Gail

Until very recently, almost all the attention in dealing with the phenomenon of CFS has been on describing the syndrome and the search for causes. Very little attention has been given to describing the recovery process, or explaining why and how people recover. Now, as we gain more experience with people going into recovery, this subject is being looked at more carefully.

Andrew Lloyd, Visiting Research Fellow at the Laboratory of Molecular Immunoregulation, National Cancer Institute, is one of the most articulate authorities on CFS research. Based on his observations of large-scale research both in his native Australia and the United States, he affirms that recovery is indeed a realistic hope:

"Our overwhelming experience . . . has been that when recovery occurs, and we believe that it happens commonly, it is complete, and one can find no evidence, pathological or hematological, of any disorder whatsoever . . . Whatever the process is that produces this fatigue state appears to be completely reversible."[1]

This perspective is reinforced by results of a study that followed the course of CFS in 135 patients in Minnesota. The study was directed by Phil Peterson, M.D., of the University of Minnesota Medical School and Hennepin County Medical Center in Minneapolis.

The results of that study led Peterson to conclude that "Although it waxes and wanes, (patients) generally head slowly out of the woods with this illness. Recovery is . . . clearly the rule in the majority of patients . . ." Peterson summarizes his perspective by stating that "This is not an interminable disability. Patients do recover gradually."[2]

We have sufficient data and clinical experience by now to say that beyond acute onset and the chronic phase, there is a recovery phase to CFS. Keeping in mind that there are wide variations among individuals, Figure 4 below represents a composite, or a general pattern of progression I have seen based on my clinical observation and the trends in the research.

Figure 4. An example of the course of CFS from onset to recovery

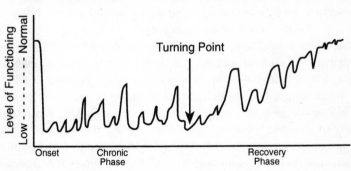

In the remainder of this chapter I will describe my observations and the findings of other researchers on the recovery phase and the factors that influence it.

The Recovery Phase

This phase can be characterized by a gradual ascent toward health, punctuated by relapses and remissions of varying degrees. While there are still these cycles, the relapses generally become less severe, of shorter duration, and with longer times between relapses.

People in the recovery phase can often point to a time when there seemed to be a positive shift or a "turning the corner" in the overall pattern of symptoms. I have heard patients attribute this shift to a variety of factors. For some it was a certain medical treatment. For others the turning point was a major change in lifestyle such as dramatically reducing work hours, quitting a stressful job, or ending a dysfunctional relationship.

Still others point to a change in their relationship with themselves, a turning inward and involvement in self-help. And in some cases there is no apparent trigger of recovery, but rather the body's healing efforts finally seem to gain the upper hand.

During the recovery phase the person learns how to carefully observe the body's signals, and to monitor its vulnerability, which is cyclical. Promotion of health remains in the foreground of daily experience. Close attention is paid to diet and stress. Many people develop a more introspective attitude toward life, with a greater appreciation for emotional honesty. As periods of remission lengthen, the person remains attentive to the body's needs and avoids the tendency to overdo. The importance of this is reinforced by occasional relapses when vigilance wanes. Gradually the person establishes a new balance of rest and activity, with a heightened sensitivity to and respect for the body. Vulnerability appears to diminish with time, as long as a vigilant attitude is maintained.

What happens at the cellular level during the recovery phase? This is an interesting question in light of our discussion in Chapter 1 about "recovery" involving a sense of living in balance and harmony. Since the symptoms are caused by the chemical by-products of an imbalanced immune response, when your symptoms diminish or disappear this is evidence that your immune system is re-establishing its own healthy balance.

When does the recovery phase end and when are you "recovered"? With some illnesses, the use of the word "recovered" is avoided, for fear of the possibility of a relapse. "In remission" or "in recovery" are preferred, at least until a substantial period of time has passed with no symptoms. With cancer, for instance, a remission of symptoms for five years is generally considered a recovery.

With CFS, however, there is no consensus on when a person is "recovered," largely due to the cyclical nature of CFS. Relapses do occur during the recovery phase, though they may be relatively minor and short-lived compared to the debilitation occurring in the chronic phase. Relapses can even occur after one has recovered a satisfactory level of functioning and a basic sense of control and balance. Again, however, these relapses are likely to be relatively mild, and serve mainly as reminders of the lessons learned during the recovery process.

Many former CFS patients have convinced me that recovery is a state that is attainable and finite, and from which you can get on with your life. Sarah, who was one of the more severe cases I have worked with, tells us:

"I consider myself fully recovered. I am able to perform all the functions that I was able to do back in 1985. My thinking is clear and my energy level is very high. I keep on top of things now by not over-doing, and this may be the key for me: I'm no longer interested in testing my limits."

As with cancer and AIDS, recovery from CFS is sustained best in people who have made profound and significant changes in their lifestyle, diet, and self-care. The degree to which relapses are possible later in life is unknown.

How Long to Recovery?

It would certainly be reassuring to have a fixed time frame for the course of CFS. This would give a sense of predictability to the experience, reducing some of the anxiety about the unknowns of it. Again, however, the tremendous variation among individuals must be taken into account.

There is slowly a consensus building among clinicians which suggests that the average duration may be around twenty-four to thirty months, but that it may be much longer for some. What we can come up with is a curve which may look something like this:

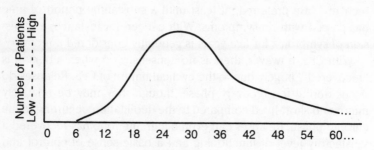

Figure 5. Months from onset to recovery (estimate)

The multicausal perspective would remind us that recovery time is affected by many different factors. These include genetic factors, self-care and self-help, medical treatment, lifestyle change, ongoing stresses, and perhaps even the individual strains of the agent(s) triggering the syndrome, the numbers or intensity of exposures to disease triggering agents, and many other factors. There are three factors, however, which stand out in predicting time to recovery: initial severity of symptoms, medical treatment, and psychological adjustment to the diagnosis.

ILLNESS SEVERITY AND RECOVERY TIME
While we are still accummulating data on this subject, evidence suggests that both the severity of your symptoms and how long you have had them may go a long way toward predicting recovery time. One of the more helpful treatments of this issue is offered by David Bell, M.D. Dr. Bell was the primary care physician in the Lyndonville, New York, outbreak of CFS in the mid 1980s, and was a collaborator in the Wistar Institute study of the possible retrovirus involved in CFS. He groups patients into three rough categories:

Group 1: mild to moderate symptoms, good prognosis for return to normal state without medical treatment.

Group 2: moderate symptoms, prolonged course (have been ill five years or longer), prominent neurological symptoms, and had a gradual onset of symptoms. These are less likely to experience remissions without medical treatment.

Group 3: severe symptoms, small chance of recovery without aggressive treatment.

Dr. Bell has offered a rating scale, based on activity level, to help in assessment of illness severity and in determining to which of the above three groups a patient might belong:

0: Entirely healthy with 100 percent activity and no symptoms
1: Increasing levels of symptoms (but greater than 75 percent activity level)
2: 75 percent activity, not able to keep up with normal level of activity
3: 50 percent reduction in activity with moderately severe symptoms (by definition, a diagnosis of CFS requires this for six months)
4: More severe reduction, with more severe symptoms (not bedridden, but well below 50 percent activity level)
5: Severely ill, bedridden

This scale is useful in helping relate the severity of illness with the course of CFS. In one study, Dr. Bell followed a group of eighteen children in the Lyndonville outbreak. The average age at onset of symptoms was eleven years. Bell reports that most of the children had reached Stage 4 or 5 on the severity scale, but most of these had returned to at least Stage 2 within three years from onset. Only a few were still in Stage 3 at the three-year mark. Interestingly, however, while all the children showed gradual improvement over the four years of the study, and most had reached Stages 1 or 2, none considered themselves completely free of the disease process (that is, reaching stage 0).[3,4]

In another study, Carol Jessop, M.D., an internist and associate professor at the University of California at San Francisco, used Bell's five-point scale to evaluate the course of 1,324 adult CFS patients between 1983 and 1990. Seventy-five percent of her sample were women, averaging 39.6 years of age.[5]

This is the largest sample studied to date. Her findings were as follows:

84 percent had recovered to Stage 0, 1, or 2, working thirty to forty hours per week.

30 percent recovered to Stage 0, considered fully recovered, which Jessop defines as eighteen months free of symptoms.

For those 30 percent, the average length of time to reach Stage 0 was twenty-nine months.

44 percent of the "recovered" patients still experienced some recurrence of symptoms with premenstrual stress, surgery, or other infections.

While these two studies dealt with very different patient samples, there is a consensus that the course of CFS is similar for children and adults. There are some generalizations we may make. One is that there is a tendency for improvement over time for most patients, although it is likely to be slower in more severe cases. The other is that even with substantial improvement, there can remain some vulnerability to symptoms, although their severity may diminish over time.

Generalizations about the course of CFS are helpful for getting a realistic perspective on what you are up against. However, the usefulness of statistics is limited when we start considering the unique individual. Obviously, statistics are based on averages of many people, and may or may not fit your personal experience.

MEDICAL TREATMENT AND RECOVERY TIME

Because research in medical treatment of CFS is in its infancy, we do not yet have data to say precisely how much particular medicines speed recovery. As Dr. Bell states, "There is a huge spectrum of disease severity in CFS, and many patients with this condition may improve to a normal functional state even without treatment."[6] Still, there is no doubt that many people with severe illness have been helped immeasurably by some of these treatments.

There are no proven "cures" so to speak. Most current treatments focus on symptoms, with varying degrees of success. It is beyond the scope of this book to discuss or recommend specific medical treatments. However, in Appendix B is an excellent summary of current treatments compiled by the CFIDS Foundation.

The types of medical treatment can be divided into four categories which are broadly outlined below.

The first are those intended to *relieve symptoms.* At this writing there is no acknowledged treatment for the most common of the symptoms, fatigue. Other symptoms do have effective treatments. While initially we may think of treating symptoms as only palliative, its importance to recovery should not be underestimated.

For example, the single most important symptom to treat is the sleep disturbance. If this is treated effectively, getting good quality rest will definitely speed the recovery process. Drugs such as tricyclic antidepressants, given in doses much smaller than would be used to treat depression itself, have been successful in treating sleep disturbance.

The pain of myalgias and arthralgias has been successfully treated with nonsteroidal anti-inflammatory drugs. Here again, to the degree that such pain impairs good quality rest, such treatment can contribute indirectly to recovery.

A second category of treatment is intended to directly intervene in the *disease process.* These treatments are mainly experimental drugs at this time, and include immune-modulators like Ampligen, whose purpose is to calm down and rebalance the immune responses. Ampligen also has antiviral properties, as do gamma globulin and Acyclovir. As more is learned about the nature of CFS and how to heal the immune system, it is likely that direct interventions like these will become more available.

Third are those treatments which deal with *related conditions.* Problems such as yeast overgrowth, intestinal parasites, and Hashimoto's thyroiditis are not uncommon in people with CFS, and can themselves contribute to chronic immune activation. Some physicians report radical improvement of CFS for patients who show evidence of these conditions and are treated for them. In addition, Dr. Jessop reports patients' cognitive disturbances have improved with appropriate treatment by anti-fungal and anti-parasitic drugs.[7]

The detection of yeast overgrowth and parasites requires the testing of both a swab sample from the rectal mucosa, and a purged stool sample. The latter is necessary because the two types of samples can give very different results. Fortunately we have effective treatments for yeast overgrowth and parasites. Testing for Hashimoto's thyroiditis requires both a thyroid function test and a thyroid antibody test. There is also effective treatment for this condition.

Fourth are treatments intended to strengthen the *overall host resistance* of the person. These include homeopathy, acupuncture, and Chinese herbs. These methods are based on their theoretical effects for enhancing and harmonizing all the body systems. This is in contrast to the other treatments which target a specific system, symptom, or pathogen.

PSYCHOLOGICAL FACTORS AND RECOVERY TIME

What role do psychological factors play in the progression to recovery? And in sustaining recovery? Can you accelerate your movement into and through the recovery phase? CFS is clearly not a psychological illness, and anyone who thinks so is sadly misinformed. Yet, it can be argued that psychological factors have the greatest impact on recovery. This is because compliance with medical treatment, lifestyle change, and self-help all originate with attitude and behavior change.

For many people the recovery phase begins with a shift of attitude in which they decide to take an active stance toward health. This often entails a radical re-evaluation of lifestyle and priorities. Typical changes have involved shifting from putting others first to acknowledging and asserting one's own needs; clearing up communication or festering conflict in relationships; altering nutritional patterns; quitting or cutting back on working hours; and setting aside time each day for self-help practices.

Often there are emotional or relationship obstacles to such changes which must be resolved. Linda, for example, reported, "The criterion I used to get healthy was: 'Whatever or whoever gives me energy, do that or be with that person. And whoever drained me, avoid them.' I absolutely had to avoid my ex-husband. I could see very clearly that ours was a toxic relationship, and that I could not be healthy and have him in my life."

Many of the principles used in coping with other illnesses apply directly to CFS. The cancer self-help movement and psychological research with cancer have given rise to the concept of the "exceptional cancer patient." This is the person who actively attempts to defy the statistics or the prognosis.

In my experience, there are exceptional CFS patients as well. They take an active role in promoting their own recovery through self-help and lifestyle change. Rather than taking the attitude that their recovery depends on medical treatment alone, they become active partners with their physicians and do what they can on their own to promote healing. As with cancer, AIDS, and other serious illnesses, the course of CFS is affected to a great degree by the coping responses of the individual.

Your attitudes and emotional state determine whether you embrace the recommended behavior and lifestyle changes, which themselves will then help lay the groundwork for your recovery. One of my patients, Sarah, states: "I believe that the gamma globulin treatment had something to do with my recovery. But I also believe that the best drugs in the world would not have worked if I'd had a pessimistic attitude. I had to believe I could get better, or that I could cope with what I had."

This perspective is reinforced by another patient, Debbie, who says, "I am convinced that the medical treatment would have not been sufficient without my changing my emotional outlook."

Making Recovery Last

As I have already stated, a classic mistake people with CFS often make is to think recovery means "returning to how I was living before I got sick." The person will seek to recreate the conditions in which illness initially developed, and will of course relapse. Many are presented with this lesson repeatedly, until they shift their criteria for what "recovery" means. It is not desirable to return to "how it was before."

The message of CFS is change. In this context, there is no turning back the clock. There is only growth, renewed sensitivity to oneself, and vigilance toward maintaining balance in living. This entails a new appreciation of the quality of life, as opposed to mere quantity.

While the person may have been able to run five miles a day before developing CFS, he may now jog two miles and savor every step, stopping without being exhausted, and appreciating the exhilaration it brings.

What is recovered is a sense of balance and control over that balance. With time he may feel able to add to the number of miles, but his orientation is now toward living in balance, rather than challenging limits.

In a practical sense, this means making conscious choices each day to pace yourself, moderate your behavior, and anticipate your vulnerability. Those who practice this kind of vigilance have shown the best success in sustaining recovery. For example, Tina, a management consultant, tells us:

"I can tell when I'm vulnerable because I get a mildly sore throat. I recognize it and I nip it in the bud before it can get established. The shift for me has been in admitting something is going on rather than being angry or denying it.

"Then I take steps to prevent relapse. If there is any stress going on, I just get myself out of it. I start taking better care of myself, get extra rest, and I can usually just skip past it. I rarely end up in bed anymore, but may just have a very mild relapse . . ."

THE BALANCING ACT
Most of us can tolerate adversity much more easily if we know it is going to pass in a predictable way, and can look forward with reasonable certainty to a time when it will be behind us. Since this is difficult with CFS, there are a variety of responses possible for coping with this uncertainty.

One is to engage in a determined quest for answers. There is, however, a risk that getting lost in this quest can be overwhelming. Attempting to stay on top of all the latest research developments, the latest scientific conferences, and the latest news stories in the media can become very time-consuming and stressful, further exacerbating symptoms. If one is not careful, it can reinforce a belief that one's deliverance from the syndrome is entirely dependent on resources *outside* oneself.

The opposite extreme, to give in to a sense of helplessness or impotence, is also detrimental. This too can add unnecessary stress to the experience of CFS. And it also reflects a belief that forces outside one's control offer the only hope for relief or help.

A third path is to *balance the quest for external support with the development of internal support.* When and if medical breakthroughs occur, this is good. In the meantime the centerpiece of your healing program must be self-empowerment.

4

Your Immune System: How It Works, and How It Is Affected in CFS

"I communicate with my immune system on a regular basis. I talk to it, and I feel it respond. I can feel a surge of energy . . ."   —Kris

In my experience with CFS patients, I have found that an understanding of certain facts about immunity is cause for hope. For once you grasp how diverse, intelligent, and resilient your body's resources are, you will be convinced that healing is entirely possible. My intention in this chapter is to offer you a practical understanding without overwhelming you with scientific jargon.

Any understanding of CFS requires an understanding of the immune system. This is because CFS is an immune-related condition in three important ways. First, the immune system is the body's frontline defense in preventing the syndrome. Second, the syndrome itself involves an impaired immune response. And third, repair of the immune response is what makes recovery last. This chapter gives an overview of what the immune system is, how it works, and how it is involved in CFS.

Overview of the Immune System

There are many ways to tell the story of immunity, and they all must grapple with its complexity. To attempt to describe the immune system requires us to artificially separate it from the rest of the body and the myriad other systems with which it relates. Of course, none of your body's systems exist in isolation. In fact, they literally flow into one another like a seamless garment, and you can not really find where one system ends and another begins. Nonetheless, I will describe what are considered to be the main elements of the immune response.

THE SEA OF MICROBES

Our environment is an ocean of life. This ocean is teaming with millions of viruses, bacteria, fungi, and other microorganisms, and this abundance of living organisms does not stop at our skin. It is normal for us to have many different kinds of organisms living inside our bodies. Some are good for us, such as certain kinds of bacteria that live in our intestinal tract and help maintain healthy digestion. Others have the potential to cause symptoms of dis-ease or imbalance in how our bodies function. These latter organisms are called pathogens.

Because our bodies are permeable, many microscopic organisms are able to penetrate our boundaries, even though we tend to think of our skin as a boundary between us and the outside world. Hence we need another level of protection *inside the body*. This is the function of the immune system—to provide internal protection from organisms or materials that penetrate our boundaries. As we shall see, the immune system is able to distinguish between friend and foe, and to protect us from materials which do not belong.

THE BALANCE OF NATURE

The notion of the balance of nature means that we are living in balance or harmony with life around us. However, it does not apply only to the grand scale of ecological crises and endangered species in the outer world. It also applies to the environment inside our bodies. In fact, many definitions of health often refer to living in balance. This implies that all of our internal life processes are somehow in harmony or rhythm with each other.

Within our bodies, as in outer nature, one of the principles for maintaining balance is that of predators and prey. Certain organisms perform the function of limiting the growth of other organisms which could upset the balance, and could ultimately lead to the demise of the entire system. In the human body this principle takes the form of the immune system hunting down and destroying pathogens. The immune system is predatory, with its white cells literally hunting down and preying upon pathogens such as viruses, bacteria, and fungi.

Because we are constantly immersed in this sea of life, it is normal for us to have these organisms within us, and it is normal for the immune system to routinely detect and destroy them, usually without our ever being even aware of it. It is normal for us to have cancer cells arise, and again, for our immune system to quietly destroy them before any noticeable pathology could ever develop. We are in a state of dis-ease when the balancing principle has somehow been interfered with or the immune system has been unable to respond as needed to maintain the balance.

With these principles in mind, let us now consider the major parts of the immune system.

THE BONE MARROW

The marrow has been used often as a powerful symbol in poetry and literature, referring to the deepest recesses of one's being. There is perhaps a universal understanding that to penetrate to the marrow is to penetrate to the core. This symbolism is certainly an accurate one when considering the human body, for without the marrow we could not live.

The marrow is a spongy tissue that fills the hollow spaces in our bones. You can think of the marrow as a vast vineyard, with billions upon billions of vines bearing fruit. The vines represent what are called stem cells. These are the cells which continuously bear fruit in the form of red cells and white cells. They give birth to the red cells and platelets of your blood. They also give birth to all your white cells, which do the work of your immune system. As these offspring of your stem cells mature and ripen, they detach and are carried out into the body by your circulatory system.

THE THYMUS GLAND

After your white cells leave the bone marrow, about half of them migrate directly to the thymus gland. The thymus is a small, walnut-sized gland located behind the breast bone. Only in recent years has it been understood as an integral part of the immune system. It serves as an incubator for certain white cells. Those cells which migrate to the thymus become "T" cells—"T" for "thymus-derived." There are basically four types of T cells, which will be discussed later. These include T-helper cells, T-suppressor cells, T-killer cells, and T-memory cells. Each of these performs a vital function in your immune system.

THE SPLEEN

The spleen is another region of spongy tissue, located deep in the abdomen between your stomach and left kidney. It too is not completely understood, but it serves as a reservoir for immune cells to be stored and to interact with each other. As we shall see later, communication among white cells is an important function of the immune system, and the spleen assists with this. Damage to the spleen can result in increased vulnerability to infection.

THE IMMUNE CELLS

Finally we have the immune cells themselves, also called white cells. There are many different types of white cells, which can be lumped into a few broad categories. If you can bear with this explanation, you will see that the immune system is an incredibly intelligent, well-organized system.

T-Helper Cells

One of the most important functions of the immune system is performed by the T-helper cell. That function is to turn on or arouse the immune response. The T-helpers receive information from other white cells that tells them of the presence of a threat. The T-helpers then release messenger molecules, called cytokines, into the bloodstream. These messages are received by the other white cells, which in turn respond with heightened activity, mounting a response to the offending material, whether it is a virus, bacteria, cancer cell, toxic substance, or other threat.

The T-helper cell is considered the trigger of the immune response. Unfortunately, it is one of the primary targets of the human immunodeficiency virus in AIDS. If the T-helper cell is injured or killed, then the person's immune response will be compromised, and they will be more vulnerable to infections. This, of course, is how AIDS becomes a life-threatening illness. People who suffer from AIDS do so as a result of infections that would not be such a threat in a normally aroused immune system.

T-Suppressor Cells

These are the cells which turn off the immune response after a threat has passed. The T-suppressors also release chemical messengers into the bloodstream to the other white cells. These chemicals have the effect of announcing that the battle is over and it is now safe to relax the defense forces and move back into a state of routine surveillance.

Immunologists have found that the ratio of T-helper cells to T-suppressor cells is an indication of the health of the immune system. The normal T-cell ratio is approximately 1.8 T-helper cells for each T-suppressor cell. This is the ratio in which the immune system is in balance and runs most harmoniously.

There are many diseases in which the ratio is out of balance, one way or the other. For instance, some lymphomas may have a ratio of 4:1 or higher, and multiple sclerosis may range from 2.5:1 to 2.8:1. AIDS, on the other hand, may be 1:1 or less, because of the toll the AIDS virus takes on T-helper cells. In the Tahoe study reported earlier, CFS patients were found to have a ratio of 3.16:1, a clearly abnormal ratio.

T-Killer Cells

There are several types of white cells which do the work of actually killing or removing unwanted material. The T-killer cell is one of these. It has receptors on its surface which receive the chemical message from the T-helper cell. The receptor is like a satellite dish, which accepts the message and processes it. After this communication has taken place, the T-killer knows what kind of target to look for and springs into action.

It is not entirely clear how T-killer cells find their targets, but it is probably through some kind of electrochemical attraction. Once they encounter the unwanted tissue, they use chemical warfare to destroy it. This means they literally come up against the surface of the offending organism and inject poison into it. The poison dissolves a hole in the wall of the offending cell, its insides spill out, and it dies. Once the battle is over, the T-killer cell receives the message from the T-suppressor to retreat, and it returns to a mode of surveillance.

T-Memory Cells

As I stated earlier, the immune system is intelligent. This means it communicates, has senses, and also has memory. The T-memory cells perform the function of storing information about past encounters with disease-causing agents. This enables the immune system to respond to an invader more quickly, because it does not have to go through the work of drawing up a profile and identification of the offender. In a sense, the information is already filed in the memory bank, enabling more rapid recognition and analysis of the offender to take place, and an overwhelming immune response may be mounted more quickly. This is the principle on which immunizations and inoculations are based.

Macrophages

As stated earlier, only about half the white cells leaving the marrow become T cells. The other half become macrophages, natural killer cells, and B cells.

Macrophages are the largest cells of the immune system. Their name literally means "the great eaters." Their function is to roam throughout the body picking up debris, digesting it, and removing it. They keep the body clean, in a sense, constantly on the look out for diseased, dying, or dead tissue. Occasionally a macrophage will encounter a pathogen such as a virus, bacterium, or other invader. When this happens, the macrophage will take a piece of material from this invader and bring this evidence to the attention of the T-memory cell for identification. In this way, macrophages play an essential role in surveillance of the body. They are also involved in eating and removing diseased or dead tissue, including the remains left by the work of killer cells.

As do all the other white cells, macrophages do have certain vulnerabilities. One is that sometimes they can be penetrated by a dangerous virus, such as HIV. In this instance, rather than killing its host cell, HIV may simply live within the macrophage and go along for the ride. Unfortunately this is one of the routes by which viruses may penetrate through the blood-brain barrier and gain entry into brain tissue. Once in the brain, they can cause symptoms. Many of the symptoms of CFS are thought to be caused by the effects of viral activity on brain tissue.

Natural Killer Cells

Natural killer (NK) cells are extremely powerful and important. They are thought to play a major role in the destruction of both cancer cells and cells which are infected by viruses.

The NK cell functions like a free spirit. Since it is not part of the T-cell network, it is not dependent on messages from the T-helpers or T-suppressors to regulate its activity. On their own, NK cells are able to detect the presence of a cancerous or virus-infected cell, and destroy it. The killing process is the same as that described earlier for the NK's close cousins, the T-killer cells.

Because they are autonomous, NK cells play an important role in diseases where T-helper function is deficient. It is believed that long-term AIDS survivors do well because their NK cells are compensating for a deficient number of T-helper cells. This demonstrates one of the important features of the immune system, called redundancy—the ability of other parts of the system to pick up the slack and compensate when one part is having difficulty. Overall, the NK cell is considered a symbol of the fighting spirit of the immune system.

B Cells

So far we have been discussing the activity of white cells which directly encounter and confront unwanted organisms—in a sense, cell-to-cell combat. Those activities described comprise what is called "cellular immunity." This refers to the activity of individual cells in defending the body directly.

There is another kind of immune activity, however, which is called "humoral immunity." Humor refers to blood, and humoral immunity involves the circulation throughout your body, of substances which are produced by your white cells.

This type of immune response is directed by B-cells. These cells tend to cluster around your lymph nodes, where they can easily monitor foreign materals, for example viruses, which may be circulating through the body. The B-cell is alerted to the presence of a virus, either by a macrophage or by T-helper cells, and rather than attacking the virus directly it begins producing antibodies for that virus. Another name for antibody is immunoglobulin (Ig). The antibodies are released into the bloodstream where they attach themselves to viruses, neutralizing them until a macrophage comes along and devours the antibody and virus together. In a sense the antibody acts like a ball and chain to the virus, rendering it unable to penetrate a cell and cause disease.

The B-cells manufacture millions of antibodies for viruses which have been detected in the body, and each type of antibody is tailor-made for a specific type of virus. Each type of virus you have been exposed to in your life is remembered by your immune system, and each has a corresponding template stored in the memory of your B-cells. Should a given virus from your past be detected again, the response of your B-cells will be swift in mounting the antibody response. Should it be an encounter with a new virus, the response will be slower because of the time needed to design the new antibodies. Finally, the B-cells respond to the level of viruses in the body, and adjust their output accordingly.

In summary, there are several qualities your immune system has which give reason for hope. These include the fact that it is intelligent, it communicates, it has memory, it has senses, and it is creative. In addition, it has certain qualities of redundancy and compensatory mechanisms—that is, it has several alternative ways of responding to a problem, and if one part of the system is having difficulty, other parts can pick up the slack.

An Open System

The immune system cannot be considered in isolation. In fact, it can be thought of as part of a larger system which could be called the healing system. This larger system also includes the mind and attitudes, the brain, the nervous system, and the endocrine system. The interaction among all these systems is the subject of the science of psychoneuroimmunology (PNI). One of the most important messages of this new field is that the immune system is an *open* system—that is, it does not act alone, but is very much influenced by communication with these other systems.

THE NEUROIMMUNE NETWORK

How does this communication take place? One of the most important insights of PNI is that the brain is a gland. As such, it releases chemicals into the bloodstream which communicate with the white cells. As mentioned earlier, white cells have receptors—like satellite dishes—on their surfaces which receive these chemical messages, decode them, and use the instructions to influence the behavior of the cell.

Another means of communication between the brain and white cells are the nerve endings reaching from the brain all the way into the bone marrow, thymus, and the other organs of the immune system. These nerve endings can stimulate the production of white cells in the marrow. They are also able to stimulate the activity of the thymus gland and other organs.

The nervous system also has *receptors* embedded in the organs of the immune system, along the walls of the blood vessels, and in the brain. These receptors are able to receive chemical messages released by the white cells, and send this information back to the brain. These signals can tell the brain about the status of the immune system and its activity. The brain can in turn respond with further release of chemicals or nerve impulses to stimulate the immune responses in the desired way. Hence there is constantly two-way communication between the immune and nervous systems.

These two modes of communication—chemical messages and nerve impulses—are the means the brain uses for mind/body communication. These are the means by which mind/body techniques such as imagery, for example, are able to influence immune activity. As we will see below, the immune system is indeed responsive to our input.

INFLUENCES ON IMMUNE RESPONSIVENESS

Your immune system's responsiveness can range along a continuum, from sluggish to hyper-active, depending upon a multitude of factors. These factors include the psychological and emotional aspects of our lives. For instance, research has shown that depression can have an adverse effect on immunity. A good example of this kind of research is a study in which NK cell activity was compared in depressed patients, schizophrenic patients, and staff in a psychiatric hospital.[1] The patients with major depressive disorder had significantly lower NK functioning than schizophrenic patients and normal controls.

Or consider the findings of a study of recently divorced people. Those who wanted the divorce, for whom it brought relief, were found to have *better* immunity than those who did not want the divorce.[2]

One of the leading authorities in the study of emotions and health is Dr. Lydia Temoshok, a health psychologist and PNI researcher with Walter Reed Army Hospital. In her highly detailed research, she found emotional expressiveness to be directly related to the thickness of tumors, as well as disease progression, in a study of fifty-nine malignant melanoma patients. In fact, emotional expressiveness turned out to be a significant predictor of the progression of melanoma.[3,4] In discussing the role of emotion in immunity and cancer progression she states, "If there is a hero in this, it's probably emotional expression."[5]

Temoshok has pioneered the notion of the "type C" personality. The qualities of a type C person include a pattern of emotional constraint, particularly in times of stress, and a sense of helplessness and hopelessness with depressive tendencies. This person is a cooperative, unassertive patient who suppresses negative emotions, particularly anger, and who accepts or complies with external authorities.[6] This is the polar opposite of the "type A" personality, which has been shown to be predictive of coronary heart disease.[7]

I would not suggest that there is such a thing as a CFS prone personality. I have seen too much diversity in the kinds of people with this syndrome. Still, it is worth considering that one's patterns of emotional expression may be a piece of the multicausal pie.

Chronic stress may be another factor. It is a widely accepted principle that stress plays a role in immunity. Specifically, certain chemicals are produced by the body when you are in a state of stress. You may recognize the "adrenalin rush" or the heightened state of alertness and perhaps strength you have when in an emergency or an anxiety-provoking situation. Indeed, there is a whole set of physiological responses taking place, which scientists call the stress response.

The chemicals produced in the stress response are both good news and bad news. The good news is that they help prepare you for fight or flight, or to function at a higher degree of effectiveness in a crisis. The bad news is that these same chemicals have a wearing or suppressing effect on your immune responses. The stress response is usually transitory, and no ill effects occur on immunity. For example, someone unexpectedly cuts in front of you on the freeway, and you may feel a very strong physiological reaction—a surge of "butterflies." But within a few minutes the reaction subsides, and by the time you reach your destination the trauma of the situation has pretty much left you.

However, if stress is chronic, then chronically suppressed immunity can of course have ill effects. In CFS both chronic stress and situational stress are of concern.

It is interesting to note that many of the studies of the stress response have studied NK cell activity and herpes viruses, such as the Epstein-Barr virus, to measure the effects of stress on immunity. These studies offer a lot of insight into the role of stress in CFS. For example, significant drops in NK cell *activity* were found in a group of seventy-five medical students during an exam period, as opposed to one month before the exams.[8]

This drop in NK cell activity was reproduced, and a significant reduction in *numbers* of NK cells was also found, in two other studies involving exam stress.[9,10]

Other immune functions are also affected by stress. A study of thirty-four first-year medical students found the percentage of T-helper cells in the blood to be significantly lower during exam periods, compared to a month earlier.[11] Likewise, a study of forty second-year medical students during final exams found similar decreases in the percentage of T-helper cells.[12]

In terms of herpesviruses, the studies of exam stress showed elevated antibody levels for the Epstein-Barr virus. Elevated antibody levels are believed to reflect poor cellular immunity in relation to the particular virus. This means that the network of T cells, NK cells, and macrophages are having difficulty keeping that virus under control. As a result, the B cells must churn out greater numbers of antibodies to compensate. Patients on immunosuppressive therapies such as cancer chemotherapy, or patients with AIDS, typically show elevated herpesvirus antibody levels.[13]

The vulnerability to herpes infections is not limited to short-term stressors like exam periods. One study followed West Point cadets for four years.[14] The cadets chosen had never had an acute EBV infection and began the study as EBV seronegative (meaning they had not yet been exposed to EBV).

Of those who became newly exposed over the four years, there was an interesting relationship between stress and how sick they became with mononucleosis, which is caused by EBV infection. The length of their hospitalization for clinical infectious mononucleosis was related to how much they had a combination of certain psychosocial stresses. Also, the amount of antibodies to EBV among those who did *not* need hospitalization was associated with those same factors. Those stresses were (1) high motivation for a military career, and (2) poor academic performance—a combination likely to create a state of chronic stress. This supports the findings of two other studies in which greater unhappiness was related to poorer control over latent herpesviruses. [15,16]

The studies cited above offer a sampling of the findings describing how stress can compromise immunity. But there is also evidence that when we feel love and joy, our immune functioning measurably improves. One study involved 132 college students to determine the effects of two kinds of emotional arousal on salivary immunoglobulin A (S-IgA) levels. S-IgA is the body's first line of defense against viruses, bacteria, or other pathogens entering through the mouth or nose.[17]

Half the students were shown the film *Triumph of the Axis in World War II.* This film was selected for its content dealing with themes of power, domination, persecution, fear, and conflict. The other half were shown the film *Mother Theresa,* a documentary of a Roman Catholic nun serving the poor, diseased, and dying in Calcutta. This film deals with themes of unconditional love, selfless service, and compassion.

Before and immediately after watching the films, the subjects' S-IgA levels were tested. There was no significant change for those who watched *Triumph of the Axis*. However, those who watched *Mother Theresa* showed significantly increased S-IgA concentrations, indicating heightened immune responsiveness.[18]

Fortunately, research in the field of PNI points the way to how we can use the pathways of mind/body communication being illustrated by all the above studies. As will be discussed in later chapters, deep relaxation and certain other self-help strategies such as meditation, imagery, and emotional expression can all take advantage of these pathways to help us heal.

While psychological states can obviously be a major influence, it is also known that nutrients can affect immunity, positively or negatively. Caffeine and refined sugar suppress the immune system, while zinc and vitamin C are among the raw materials of which it is constructed, and which it requires to perform.

We will discuss the enhancement of immunity at greater length later. For now, the conclusion I invite you to consider is this: because your immune system is an *open* system, there is potential for you to have an impact on your healing process by how you choose to live each day.

Types of Immune-Related Illness

With this explanation of the immune system, let us now turn our attention to the various types of illness to which it responds. This will help give us a perspective on CFS in relation to other illnesses. There are four broad types of immune-related illness.

TYPE ONE

One involves an *insufficient* immune response to an *external* pathogen, such as in a viral or bacterial infection. The pathogen enters the body and is not met with an appropriate immune response. Either the immune system is suppressed for some reason, or the pathogen is somehow able to deceive the immune system and slip through the defenses. This is thought to be the case in HIV, for example, where the virus changes form and keeps a step ahead of the immune system's ability to manufacture appropriate antibodies. In more common viral conditions, however, the immune response follows a normal course, and after an initial flare-up, it catches up with the numbers of viruses and eliminates them from the body.

TYPE TWO

A second type of illness is where there is an *insufficient* response to an *internal* pathogen, such as cancer cells. In this case, the cancer cells are growing and reproducing at a rate faster than the immune system is recognizing and destroying them. Again, the problem may be related to suppressed immunity, but it also may be related to some cancer-causing substance simply overwhelming the body's ability to respond.

TYPE THREE

The third type of illness involves an *overactive* response to an *external* pathogen. This occurs in allergies and food sensitivities, where the immune system misinterprets a substance as being harmful to the body when in fact it is not. As a result it is fighting an unnecessary battle, and the by-products of this battle create unpleasant symptoms.

TYPE FOUR

Finally, some illnesses involve an *overactive* immune response to *internal* tissues. These are called autoimmune diseases. Here again, the immune system is malfunctioning and mounting a misguided attack against the body's own healthy tissues. This occurs in multiple sclerosis, rheumatoid arthritis, lupus, and Graves' disease, for example.

CFS: A Disease in Search of a Category

Where does CFS fit in? Interestingly, CFS does not fit neatly into any of the above types of illness. Rather, it has some of the qualities of each. This is one of the reasons why mainstream medicine has had such reluctance to acknowledge the syndrome as a distinct disease—it simply does not fit any of our familiar categories.

While the involvement of the nervous system is a major part of the syndrome, the heart and soul of making a diagnosis, according to Dr. Paul Cheney, remain to be immunologic testing. He describes "all manner of unusual phenomena" going on in the great majority of patients. The most common pattern is chronically heightened T-cell activation, elevated levels of cytokines such as interferon and interleukin II, immunoglobulin deficiencies, and severe natural killer (NK) cell functional deficiency.[19] In fact, NK cell dysfunction is so central to the condition that in Japan the disease is called "Low NK Syndrome."[20]

One leading CFS immunologist, Nancy Klimas, M.D., of the University of Miami, believes this NK deficiency is a central feature of CFS, and qualifies the syndrome as an acquired immune deficiency. She states that her findings, based on a patient population of 500, show higher than normal *numbers* of natural killer cells in CFS, as if the immune system is trying to respond to something, but very low *functionality*. The ability of those NK cells to kill was the lowest of any group studied, including among people in early stages of HIV infection, people with ARC (AIDS-Related Complex), and in intravenous drug users.[21]

According to Dr. Klimas, "The most compelling finding was that natural killer cell cytotoxicity (*functionality*) in chronic fatigue syndrome was as low as we have seen in any disease . . . These cells seem to feel the way that CFS patients do—they're exhausted."[22] Other researchers have observed that NK cell *numbers* rise during the acute stage of CFS, and then return to normal after recovery.[23]

The findings about immune-system irregularities help explain why viruses such as Epstein-Barr (EBV), cytomegalovirus (CMV), human herpesvirus number 6 (HHV6), herpesvirus types I or II, or others can show more activity in the person with CFS.

THE REAL CAUSE OF SYMPTOMS
These immune dysfunctions are part of a broader picture which also includes immune system *up-regulation*. It is the chronic, high state of immune activation that appears to be the real cause of most of the symptoms. They are caused by the chemical by-products being churned out by the immune system.

Some of those products, the cytokines, are known to be potent virus- and cancer-fighters. However, they also cause the very symptoms people with CFS have. In cancer, research has shown that some of these substances have been an effective treatment for certain cancers. They include interleukin I and II, and interferon, well-known cancer treatments. The cancer research also shows, however, that patients using these treatments can expect certain side effects, *which go away when treatment is discontinued.* These side effects, which cancer patients are told to expect, *fit the symptom picture of CFS almost perfectly.*

In fact, Dr. Klimas and her colleagues have identified a cytokine abnormality that has not been seen before in any disease. In about 35 percent of their patients, they are seeing interleukin-1 (IL-1) levels that are *50 times* higher than normal. Klimas reports that in studies of mice with similarly high levels, the mice develop muscle weakness, lassitude, generalized inflammation, cardiac tachycardia, decreases in cardiac output, and peripheral neuropathies—all symptoms found in severe cases of CFS.[24]

Dr. Jay Levy of the University of California, San Francisco, considered by many as the first to have actually located and isolated the AIDS virus, has proposed that the syndrome be renamed "Chronic Immune Activation Syndrome."[25] It is indeed unfortunate that the syndrome was named for merely one of its many symptoms, fatigue, rather than being given a name which represents more accurately the disease process itself. Paul Cheney, M.D., has made the comment that this is like calling pneumonia "chronic cough syndrome."[26]

According to Levy: "We believe that there is an infectious agent that enters the host and activates the immune system . . . some individuals, because of their genetic makeup or because of their state at the time of infection, will not be able to turn off that activated state . . . (and) the immune system never returns to a normal resting state. So, these people are in a state of chronic immune activation."[27]

If the retrovirus being studied by Dr. DeFreitas at the Wistar Institute and by Dr. Martin at USC is found to be the culprit, it may be that it triggers the disturbance in the immune system and then is either eliminated or goes into hiding, leaving behind a disturbed immune response. One theory is that it is some kind of a hit-and-run virus, leaving the immune system firing away at no specific target.

BREAKING THE RULES

As we can see from this discussion, CFS has elements of all four major categories of immune-related illness, as illustrated in Figure 6 below. With regard to *insufficient response to an external pathogen,* most likely it involves a virus entering the body from the environment. The immune system has not successfully defended against the invader. The virus gets a foothold, penetrating certain immune cells, and triggers the dysregulation.

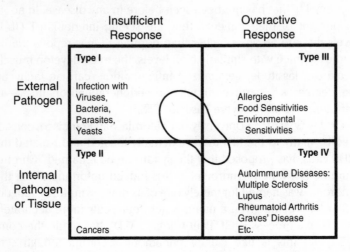

	Insufficient Response	Overactive Response
External Pathogen	**Type I** Infection with Viruses, Bacteria, Parasites, Yeasts	**Type III** Allergies Food Sensitivities Environmental Sensitivities
Internal Pathogen or Tissue	**Type II** Cancers	**Type IV** Autoimmune Diseases: Multiple Sclerosis Lupus Rheumatoid Arthritis Graves' Disease Etc.

Figure 6. Types of immune-related illness: CFS (encircled area) in search of a category

The second category, *insufficient response to an internal pathogen,* generally relates to the growth and spread of cancer cells. CFS has been linked statistically to a slightly increased incidence of certain kinds of cancer such as Burkitt's lymphoma and nasopharyngeal carcinoma. This by no means implies, however, that people with CFS are in general at greater risk of cancer. At this stage of our knowledge, it is simply an interesting statistical association.

With regard to the third category, *overactive response to external pathogens,* people with CFS typically have increased problems with allergies, and may even have a totally new onset of allergies. An allergic response is an extreme immune response. Sensitivities to foods and other substances in the environment such as perfumes, smoke, paint, carpeting, and certain construction materials create serious problems for CFS patients, all as a result of the immune system's heightened sensitivity.

With regard to the fourth category, *overactive response to internal tissues,* the immune system is not targeting the host's tissues as it would in more common autoimmune diseases. However, the chemical by-products of the disease process do adversely affect neurological tissue in many patients, causing brain lesions and serious disability. It is only in this indirect sense that CFS has some semblance to an autoimmune disease. If the areas of the brain that are damaged are involved in regulation of the immune response, then it is even more difficult to restore the proper relationships between these two systems, and a pattern of chronic illness results.

CFS and AIDS

The question often arises as to whether CFS has any association with AIDS. This is a logical question, because both conditions involve difficulties in immune functioning. However, in reality they are very different syndromes. CFS is actually opposite to HIV in terms of immune system activation. To compare the two is like comparing apples and oranges. The symptoms in CFS are *directly* caused by the *over-*activity of the immune system, flooding the body with toxins which have ill effects. In AIDS, the symptoms are *in*directly caused by the *under-*activity of the immune system, allowing what would normally be innocuous infections to take hold.

The Good News

CFS presents us with a unique challenge. We must abandon many of our old concepts of health and illness, and rededicate ourselves to the quest for understanding how harmony can be restored among multiple bodily systems.

The good news is that in spite of our limited understanding and our lack of a medical cure, people do recover their health. The fact that many have recovered in the absence of medical treatment is evidence that the body has the inherent ability to heal such immune dysfunction. The cells and tissues of the immune system, because of their genetic programming, remember what harmony is and how to restore it. It takes time. Medical treatment and lifestyle change can accelerate the healing process, but the resiliency and intelligence of the immune system are what make such healing possible.

PART II

The Path of Self-Empowerment

5

Coping with Your Symptoms

"I have a choice. Either I listen to the signs that my body gives me, however minor they might seem, or I don't. The longer I don't listen, the higher the likelihood of ending up with a full-blown relapse."
—Adriana

In this chapter we will explore ways of coping with specific symptoms of CFS. This material will be complemented by the next chapter, in which we will broaden our focus to the more general issues of how to change your overall lifestyle to promote recovery.

Before we deal with specific strategies, there is something more basic which must first be addressed: *your overall perspective* toward the illness. At the heart of how you cope is *how you think* about the syndrome, and about your *ability to respond* to it. Psychologists call this your "appraisal" of the situation. How you appraise the situation determines the range of options you recognize for handling it.

It is quite common for people with CFS to have the attitude that, in the absence of a medical cure, this is the beginning of a miserable decline to an agonizing and painful demise. You could believe yourself to be powerless in the face of this condition, and that your only salvation is to await years of research until a medical cure is found. With this point of view, coping is just a matter of trying to cut your losses, to minimize your suffering, and not much else can be accomplished. Your efforts to cope with symptoms may carry a feeling of despair, helplessness, or desperation, and may actually bring more anxiety into your life.

On the other hand, you might embrace the attitude that the symptoms and the illness are transitory, and that there is hope for recovery. In this case, there will be less anxiety around the symptoms. You might appraise yourself as having some power to influence your health. You might view CFS as a challenge rather than a sentence. In this case, you may have more optimistic expectations, and your emotional state will be very different.

The self-empowerment approach in CFS is based on this latter kind of thinking. There is a shift away from the old medical model in which you are a helpless victim dependent on medical breakthroughs. Instead, you can think of yourself as capable of impacting your illness with self-help strategies and lifestyle changes. In short, you can have what psychologists call an "internal locus of control." This means that what happens to you is controlled by *you* rather than by circumstances outside of you.

A Primer on Stress and Coping

Imagine you are walking across the floor in your room. As you walk, notice how each step is a process of maintaining balance. You keep yourself balanced from front to back, as well as from side to side, and this comes so automatically you usually don't think much about it.

Now imagine that you are carrying a heavy suitcase in one hand. This tends to pull you off balance, and you have to lean your body in the opposite direction to maintain balance. The weight is pulling on your arm and shoulder, and strain develops in your muscles. You have to alter your pattern of walking to accommodate these effects. In order to keep your balance across the room you have to compensate for the suitcase.

In this example, the suitcase represents what we could call a "stressor" (a cause of stress), and your efforts to compensate represent "coping." All the symptoms of CFS are stressors. The syndrome causes imbalance in all areas of life, including your emotions, all your bodily systems, your relationships, your patterns of work, play, and rest; and your self-concept. Some of the symptoms are successfully treated by medication and some are not. Some can be helped by behavior strategies, and others cannot.

You need to know what you can do to reduce symptoms. But what about when nothing works? You also need to know how to maintain a sense of *inner* peace or balance when there is no solution that really changes the symptom.

As a result, psychologists speak of two kinds of coping. The first is what you do to change the *problem,* in this case the symptom. The second is what you do to handle your *emotional reactions* to the problem, such as the frustrations, fears, or feelings of helplessness about the symptom.

Leaning away from the suitcase is an example of responding to the problem itself, what is called "problem-focused" coping. You could also just set the suitcase down and refuse to carry it. You may choose to hire someone to carry it for you. Or you might empty some of the contents of the suitcase and make a couple of trips. These are all strategies to handle the situation, reducing the stress it causes.

However, you may not always be able to change the situation. If you are carrying your suitcase to the bus stop and can't afford to miss your bus, you may have to go on carrying it and endure the stress. In other words, you handle the stress not by changing the situation, but by changing your inner experience of it. You may tell yourself that you only have a few feet to go, you'll be able to rest once you get there, and it will be worth the effort because your rich uncle is meeting you at the other end of the trip.

This inner dialogue or understanding helps you cope with the stress by maintaining a sense of equilibrium on an emotional level. This is what we mean by "emotion-focused" coping. You have changed your perspective on the symptom. You have changed its *meaning.* Then, rather than going into anger, despair, or frustration, you go through the experience relatively peacefully.

Very often, people with CFS try to put all their effort into problem-focused coping. They spend a great deal of energy searching for external solutions, medical breakthroughs, or promising new treatments. However, since many symptoms do not have effective solutions, this relentless quest can lead to a great deal of frustration, depletion of energy, and a sense of hopelessness. There needs to be a balance between our *outer* efforts to resolve the symptoms, and our *inner* efforts to have a sense of emotional well-being, harmony, and balance.

Below we will look at the major types of symptoms of CFS, and alternative ways to cope with them. You will see that both emotion-focused and problem-focused strategies can be essential at different times.

Fatigue

In managing the fatigue, it helps if you can be familiar with your own cycles and patterns. These may or may not be obvious to you. One way to establish them is to keep a log of your energy levels: first for the hours of the day, and second, your broader patterns over several days and weeks. You might simply use a scale from one to ten as a way of recording energy levels and seeing patterns.

By watching your patterns, you may see that at times the fatigue is connected to an activity where some exertion took place. Or you may find it affected by where you are in your menstrual cycle. At other times, the fatigue may seem to come out of the blue, even when you have been taking excellent care of yourself. Such is the cyclical and sometimes unpredictable nature of the syndrome. But in general, you should discover that there is a somewhat predictable pattern of relative highs and relative lows over time.

Once you get a good sense of your patterns, you can begin working with them. There are some "dos" and "don'ts" to this. The biggest "don't" is to challenge your limits. Respect your body's cycles.

On your good days, you must respect the fact that your body remains vulnerable. You must learn to pace yourself. Yet, as you are probably aware, there is a tremendous temptation to test limits and overdo on the good days. After all, you might think, "I don't know how long this high is going to last, and I've got so much I want to do while I have the chance. I'd like to wash the car, go shopping, go to a movie, clean the carpet, vacuum the draperies, clean out the refrigerator, mow the lawn, go to the beach . . ." And then, of course, you crash.

THE FIFTY-PERCENT SOLUTION

Virtually every person I have known with CFS can relate to this experience. I have, however, found an effective way to work *with* energy patterns rather than against them. I call it "the fifty-percent solution," and it has proven very helpful for many patients. It goes as follows: When you find yourself on a good day or in a period of remission, make an assessment of how much you feel you can do. For example, though up to now you have been able to exercise only very little, you may feel confident that you can walk a half mile with no problem. Following this method, you would walk a quarter mile, and then stop. Then for the next day or two, you very closely observe the impact this has had on your body.

If you relapse, your assessment must be adjusted downward on your next good day. If you feel fine, you may repeat this process a few times, each time limiting yourself to 50 percent of what you feel capable of doing. As your confidence grows, you may feel capable of walking a mile, in which case you would try a *half* mile, followed again by a close monitoring of your body's responses. Never take the attitude of challenging your limits.

The essence of the fifty-percent solution is that you are spending half the energy you feel is available, and you are *investing the other half* in your body's healing process. It takes energy to heal. Energy that is spent outwardly is not available inwardly to energize your healing process. You are investing in a savings program that collects interest. Let your wealth grow, rather than spending every penny you find in your pocket.

It takes some self-discipline to hold back in this way. But, to borrow a phrase from the field of psychiatry, a "flight into health" is often followed by a relapse. The strengthening of your resistance takes time and patience.

As you move further toward recovery, your assessment of your available energy will gradually rise. As you continue observing the fifty-percent solution on your good days, you will discover that your periods of remission lengthen, and that the severity of your relapses gradually diminishes.

Recovery demands that you tune in to your body and truly respect the need to pace yourself. The fifty-percent solution has served as a useful guideline for many along the road to healing.

MEDITATION AND RELAXATION

Beyond the fifty-percent solution and metering out your energy, some patients find meditation as a help with fatigue. The restorative power of meditation is that it lowers tension and agitation, and it leads to the relaxation response. As Harold, a high school math teacher, reports, "I would meditate once a day in the afternoon, about half an hour to forty-five minutes, as a calming device. That would tend to take some of the fatigue and muscle shakes away."

Why does this work? If we accept that the fatigue and muscle shakes are symptoms arising from immune hyperactivation, then something about the meditation must be having a moderating effect on the immune system. The relaxation response has a harmonizing and rebalancing effect on the immune system, and meditation is a direct path to this healing state. This will be covered in more detail in Chapter 8.

Handling Cognitive Symptoms

CFS is very much, perhaps primarily, a neurological condition. It results in disturbed cognition—that is, difficulties in thinking. As I've noted, this can take the form of problems with memory, problem solving, forgetfulness, mental confusion, concentration, finding words, and a wide range of other signs of impaired mental functioning. An overall strategy for handling this array of symptoms is twofold.

First is to have a realistic perspective on what is happening. Remind yourself that you are experiencing symptoms and that you are not crazy. Remember that symptoms are transitory. Having a regular dialogue with your inner child may be very helpful for reinforcing this awareness (discussed in Chapter 11). Second, use strategies that help you compensate for the symptoms.

Following are some examples of strategies people have used to cope with the cognitive dysfunction.

Harold shows us a good example of using self-talk to maintain perspective. He states: "I developed an inability to read or do any kind of figuring. I couldn't even write a check, add or subtract. It was demoralizing. At first I thought 'I'm so stupid, what's wrong with me?' But then I realized, 'No, this is not my fault, it's just another part of the disease,' and so I could cope with it. I learned to take a lot more notes, not to write checks, and not to try reading things I couldn't comprehend."

Joanne, a management consultant, also discovered the benefits of talking to herself: "In my work I usually had to juggle a lot of things at once. With CFS I had to start writing everything down. At first I resented it, because I was used to having such a good memory. The other thing I had to do was talk to myself out loud, which would help me remember what I was doing. I would also read out loud to help retain what I was reading."

Mark, a physician, tells of how he handled the problem of forgetting patients' names: "I started taking photographs of them. New patients would come in and we'd just take a picture and put it in their chart. I'd remember their situation better by looking at the picture than by their name . . ."

Here are some other ways of handling cognitive symptoms:

Become an expert list-maker. Make a list each morning of what you need to do that day. Make other lists to keep track of tasks, appointments, etc.

Use time schedules and calendars to keep track of your activities each day.

Wear a watch that beeps on the hour if you need help keeping track of time.

Use lots of Post-its around your home or workplace to help you keep track of things you need to remember.

Use repetition: when being told new information, repeat it to yourself several times to help lay down the memory.

Write notes to yourself, and take notes when having important conversations with people.

Before you call someone, make a note to yourself about who you are calling and what you need to say.

Keep calculators handy.

Play board games or use other activities to stimulate your mind and keep it active.

Practice speaking more slowly, not being in a hurry to choose your words.

When driving, try to have someone with you who can serve as a backseat driver.

There is a kind of therapy called "cognitive restructuring" which is of great benefit in handling the cognitive problems. Cognitive restructuring as applied to CFS has been pioneered by Linda Miller Iger, Ph.D., of the Chronic Fatigue Syndrome Institute of Beverly Hills, California. This approach is especially helpful in improving memory loss. Examples of cognitive restructuring are "mnemonic devices" such as:

Acrostics: creating sentences with words that all begin with the same letter ("Make mail Monday morning")

Acronyms: making a word out of the first letter of several words ("RAMBO—Remember Afternoon Medication B_{12} Oral")

Training in cognitive restructuring usually takes place over several sessions, with a qualified psychotherapist. Not all are trained in this, so you will have to ask around to find a good resource for this approach.

Having loved ones, friends, and associates help can be very important in handling cognitive symptoms. These people are in a position to remind you of appointments or tasks, to help you with strategies listed above, and to reinforce your efforts to maintain your own balance. In some cases, having a support system by phone has made a great difference in people's staying on a schedule and remembering to complete necessary tasks such as taking medication.

Emotional Disturbance

There are two distinct sources of emotional disturbance in CFS. One is the "somato-psychic" aspect of CFS—the fact that the disease process affects the neurological system, altering brain chemistry and, consequently, emotions. The other source of distress is the psychological experience of having to adjust to life with a chronic illness. It is impossible to say how much of the emotional disturbance in one individual is attributable to the disease process, and how much is the psychological reaction. And of course, the two can feed on each other—as in "I'm depressed about being depressed."

As I've mentioned, the most common emotional symptoms are anxiety, panic attacks, depression, mood swings, shortness of breath; and personality changes, such as increased volatility, emotional sensitivity, or emotional withdrawal.

EXPRESSING FEELINGS

What are the keys to handling these kinds of disturbance? The most fundamental answer is expressing your feelings. This of course can be done in several ways, such as:

Talk about your feelings with a confidant or in a support group.
Talk with yourself in private, letting all your inner voices be heard.
Cry or use other means of nonverbal expression.
Draw images that express how you feel.
Write about your feelings in a journal.

All of these are excellent ways to express. In addition to releasing emotional tension, such expression also helps rebalance your hormonal system. Most likely you have experienced the feeling of relief or uplift that comes when you confide a secret or a strong feeling in another. The "good feeling" that comes from this is the actual result of the hormonal shift in your body back toward balance.

Dr. James Pennebaker, Professor of Psychology at Southern Methodist University, has made a study of the health effects of expressing traumatic feelings. In one study, fifty participants were instructed to write in a journal for twenty minutes per day for four consecutive days. Half were told to write about the most traumatic events of their lives. The other half wrote about superficial topics like the weather. Both groups gave blood samples before and after the study. Six weeks later, the first group showed significantly higher T-cell responsiveness and significantly fewer health clinic visits than the comparison group.[1] This is one of the first studies to link emotional expression with both immunity and health status.

BREATHING

Another key to maintaining emotional equilibrium is conscious breathing. This is of particular importance in CFS since shallow breathing will exacerbate your emotional upset and contribute to anxiety or panic attacks.

Full abdominal breathing will dramatically change your emotional experience. More energy will be available in your body. Tension will be more easily released. The body will sense that there is ample energy available. It will not go into feelings of anxiety that occur naturally when it is deprived of adequate oxygen. We will explore breathing further in Chapter 10.

HANDLING ANXIETY OR PANIC ATTACKS

I like to emphasize that although anxiety attacks are a symptom of CFS, you can empower yourself to control or prevent them. I have heard many patients report that they had no idea how shallow their breathing was, and that in their anxiety or panic attacks, they realized they had stopped breathing and were literally holding their breath.

One of my patients, Gail, found that breathing made the difference in her controlling anxiety attacks. "It took a lot of practice, but I learned that when I felt one coming on, I could consciously start taking deep breaths. Sometimes I would conjure up an image that helped me relax, and the breathing and imagery together really helped. I also used relaxing music, and eventually I found I would have the attacks less frequently. I got hooked on relaxation."

Another patient, Sharon, reported: "I didn't have a lot of panic attacks, but the few that I had were very scary. Most were when I was a passenger in a car. I handled them by closing my eyes so that I couldn't see anything around me. I just trusted the fact that we would get to wherever we were going. I was able to talk about what was happening. I'd tell my husband, 'I'm very anxious right now, I'm panicky, I'm frightened. I understand what's happening. I'm going to close my eyes and relax and breathe.' I was relieved to find out that this was not an isolated symptom for me, but was something that other people were experiencing too, and it was all part of the syndrome."

SUICIDAL THOUGHTS AND FEELINGS

Not surprisingly, when suicidal thoughts or feelings arise, the most helpful thing you can do is express them. This is a time when interpersonal support is especially important. Ask for physical contact and the moral support you need from those who care about you.

Consider Laurel's example: "I thought about suicide. I was getting a divorce, and everything was going wrong—my health, my business, my finances—and I didn't think I'd ever get well. I thought, 'What good is life if I can't provide for myself? Even if someone takes care of me, why lie around in a body like this, sick, lonely, and unable to think of a way out?' I didn't try it, but suicide was very attractive to me. The most positive step I took was to open up to my friend about it. We talked on the phone several times a week, and we invited God in to participate in a healing process. This was the beginning of my recovery."

Preferably, there is another person with whom you can share this, but if not, at least write about these feelings in a journal. The simple act of putting these feelings into words, while not completely eliminating the feelings, will bring about some relief. Through such expression, some of the emotional charge will be released and it will be easier to put the feelings into perspective as the transitory symptom that they are.

Reminding yourself that the suicidal thoughts or feelings are transitory and symptomatic of the illness helps you get through those times when you can't see any way out. But if suicidal feelings or ideas persist, then you should talk them over with a professional therapist who is informed about CFS. Beyond that you may need to consult your physician to consider medication to help you through this crisis.

In coping with the emotional symptoms, it is very important to remind yourself that you are not crazy, and that this is a symptom of your illness. As with the cognitive disturbances, having a dialogue with your inner child will help soften the fears. It may also be helpful for you and loved ones to enter into counseling with a professional who is informed about CFS and can help you all communicate and express more openly.

Sleep Disturbance

As stated earlier, the sleep disturbance is in a sense the most important symptom to manage. This is because in order for the body's self-repair mechanisms to function, quality rest is needed. The sleep disturbance can be either an inability to sleep (insomnia) or inability to stay awake (hypersomnia). Fortunately, many patients have been helped with very low doses of anticonvulsant or antidepressant medication (much lower than would be used to treat psychiatric depression).[2]

One common problem is that patterns or cycles of sleep may vary. In this case, you should gently try to accommodate the body's preferred sleep pattern rather than trying to force it to follow a certain schedule. Sleep when it is easiest, even though this may be at less conventional times.

A wide variety of other strategies have been used with varying success by different people. They range all the way from drinking water or herbal tea before bed, to experimenting with various foods which may help you relax and sleep, taking a warm bath, and simply reading. Through trial and error, you can develop your own unique routine, almost like a ritual, of what works for you.

Enrolling the support of family or loved ones can be a real help, as described by Delores: "My family protects my sleep. I can't get up at six in the morning. It makes my day too long. My husband has been wonderful about it. He gets the kids off to school quietly, and then I wake up on my own when my body's ready to. If I wake up by an alarm, my body gets very upset—it's that delicate. Also, we turn off the phone every night."

Finding ways to shut off the mind in order to sleep is difficult for many people with CFS. Because of the neurological arousal and agitation caused by the syndrome, even though the body is exhausted, the mind may keep on going and keep you awake.

One of the most helpful things you can do is to practice meditation and deep relaxation techniques (see Chapter 8). This will help to calm the mind and reduce the degree of neurological arousal.

The amount of sleep needed is less in people who meditate, because the mind itself is a tremendous consumer of energy. The state of relaxation induced by meditation is not exactly the same as sleep, but it is very good quality rest for the body. It may not calm the mind completely, but at least it will reduce the portion of agitation or arousal caused by the worry and anxiety of not being able to sleep well.

Sensory Dysfunction

The wide variety of sensory dysfunctions can be dealt with in a variety of ways. The basic rule of thumb is to modify your environment to minimize the amount of invasive stimuli surrounding you.

For light sensitivity, you may need to take steps to reduce the intensity of light in your home. For example, replace light bulbs with a lower wattage. When going out, you may need to wear sunglasses, and may even need to wear them indoors.

To reduce the effects of loud noises, you may want to wear earplugs, especially while sleeping. While driving, you may choose to keep the car windows up to avoid being shocked and distracted by noise from other vehicles. A horn can, of course, be anxiety-provoking, especially if it comes from three lanes away but sounds like it is next to you. You may also prefer to drive or ride in cars with the radio off.

For eye sensitivity, some people find cool packs or warm packs helpful for relieving the discomfort. Reading creates special problems for many people with CFS. This involves not only the challenge of concentration, but also focusing the eyes and tracking across the page, while remaining on the same line. Linda Miller Iger, Ph.D., of the Chronic Fatigue Syndrome Institute of Beverly Hills, recommends the novel idea of using a reading prosthesis. This is a card you can make from a note card or part of a cardboard box. You cut it to the width of a page of type, with a slit cut in the center. The slit is about a line and a half high, and allows you to move down the page and read one line at a time. In addition you may want to try using a three-paneled barrier around the page to prevent outside visual distractions while reading.

Another kind of sensory dysfunction many experience is a much greater allergic responsiveness and sensitivity to environmental toxins, odors, chemicals, or medicines. This is actually an immune over-reaction, in which the immune system itself has the sensory dysfunction. In this case, you need to make your physical environment as non-toxic as possible. Steps you can take:

Use non-toxic and natural cleaning materials.
Refrain from use of scented toiletries.
Ask people around you to observe the above suggestions.
Stay away from new construction materials which are still releasing out-gases from glues, paints, etc. Glues are a special problem, and they are present in carpeting, plywood, and many manufactured wood items.

As with most other symptoms, you will probably find that your sensitivities wax and wane, depending on how much quality rest you have been able to achieve and where you are in your cycles with the syndrome.

Physical Pain

There is a great deal of individual variation in terms of remedies for the pain. Medically, people have been helped with arthralgias (joint pain) and myalgias (muscle pain) by the use of non-steroidal and anti-inflammatory drugs.[3] In terms of self-help, some respond well to heat, while others are aggravated by it. This apparently depends on whether the pain is caused by muscle stiffness or the inflammatory autoimmune reaction. If it is the latter, then heat will stimulate a broader immune response, creating more inflammation, which you do not want.

Some people are helped by applying ice to the tender points. Some are helped with mild exercise, while others are made worse by exercise. Yoga-type stretching is helpful for some, and walking for others. Because of the range of individual responses, you will need to experiment to find what works for your type of pain.

Gastrointestinal Difficulties

Some of the digestive disturbance may be due to the effects of viral activity on the tissues lining the digestive tract. This is why it is important to work with a physician who is informed about CFS should you seek medical help for the digestive problems.

As mentioned earlier, it is important to be tested for yeast overgrowth and parasites. Beyond that, by paying close attention to your body's reactions you can determine your food sensitivities or allergies, and avoid those foods. Many people have found that their sensitivities and allergies disappear after clearing up their yeast overgrowth.

In general, a relatively bland, whole foods, natural diet is usually recommended. This of course means avoiding sugar, caffeine, chocolate, and foods laced with a lot of preservatives and artificial ingredients. This way there is less of a burden placed on the immune system while it is in its healing process.

Many people with CFS experience weight changes as a result of fluctuations in their metabolism caused by the disease process. Some have found that the weight changes have endured beyond recovery, whether they are considered desirable or not. This may mean adjusting to a new body image as heavier or lighter than before. It is important not to stress your body in trying to reclaim a prior image of yourself if that is not what your body wants to do. If necessary, supportive counseling can help you develop a more friendly, accepting relationship with your body. Care should be taken to work with medical supervision if you decide to alter your diet because the weight changes are unacceptable.

Cardiac Symptoms

To reiterate what we said in Chapter 2, the consensus among CFS experts is that the cardiac symptoms usually do not represent serious coronary problems. Still, it is wise to rule out any more serious heart conditions.

In terms of self-help, the practice of deep relaxation and full breathing will contribute to greater calm and a more even heart rate. When you find yourself having the common heartbeat irregularities, it is easy to add more stress to the situation with a fear response about what it means. Remind yourself that this is a symptom, and that you can handle it by taking some time to go into abdominal breathing and relaxation.

Also, upon consultation with your physician, you may find that magnesium deficiency is a factor, in which case supplementation will help with these symptoms.

Other Symptoms and Alternative Treatments

In this discussion we have, of course, only addressed the main types of symptoms, and there are countless other symptoms possible. As with those discussed here, severity and remedies vary from one individual to the next.

In managing the symptoms, you do not have to go it alone. You can see yourself as in a partnership with your health-care practitioner. In addition to conventional (allopathic) medicine, there are other approaches to medicine which have had varying success with symptoms in CFS. The techniques of mind/body medicine being presented in this book have been of great benefit to countless patients. Also, people have received symptomatic relief using a whole range of other therapies, including acupuncture, acupressure massage, herbal medicine, naturopathic medicine, homeopathy, hydrotherapy, colon therapy, and other less mainstream approaches. Ultimately you have to trust your intuition and inner guidance to steer you to resources that you feel may help you.

If you decide to explore alternatives, you need not see yourself as having to choose between mainstream and alternative therapies. Rather, you can use a variety of therapies that *complement,* rather than compete with, each other. One fact about CFS is very clear: no one approach has all the answers.

"This Too Shall Pass"

The journey through CFS can bring many moments in which nothing seems to help, and you feel utterly hopeless and full of despair. What can you do to make it through those times of hitting bottom?

Remind yourself that the illness and its symptoms are *transitory.* One of history's greatest psychologists, Gautama Buddha, taught about the principle of "impermanence." His message was that all that we think is real and lasting eventually passes. Usually this understanding is applied to our attachment to material possessions, relationships, or to experiences that we think will bring us contentment. It applies equally, however, to suffering. Nothing lasts forever, not suffering, not the symptoms of CFS, and not CFS itself. Closing your eyes and repeating the affirmation "this too shall pass" has been used for thousands of years as a way for people to gain a sense of detachment from suffering.

Another source of help in those moments is to find something to distract your attention away from the symptoms. Melva tells us: "When I find myself in a state of discouragement, I *do something*. I turn on a relaxation tape, meditate, or look for laughter. I might flick through the TV channels to find a funny program—anything to focus my mind away from my illness."

Remember: symptoms pass. People do recover from CFS. Brain lesions do disappear. People have been able to jog, surf, and ski again. There is life after CFS. The symptoms are not something to fight with, they are a natural expression of the illness, and are transitory. As you learn more about your patterns of symptoms, you will gradually be able to reduce their severity and may even prevent some of them. In the next chapter we will explore how to develop an overall lifestyle which will help you to promote your recovery.

6

Changing Your Lifestyle to Promote Recovery

"I want to get rid of this thing as fast as I can, because I've got so much work to do."   —Joanne

All the experts agree, especially in the absence of a medical cure, that lifestyle change is the necessary foundation for recovery from CFS. According to Paul Cheney, M.D., this is "easily the most important and often the least emphasized" part of treatment.[1] And the body itself, if it too could be considered an expert on what it needs, seems to be saying the same thing. The illness demands dramatic and sometimes painful decisions to change one's way of life. In this chapter we will take a thorough look at all the areas of lifestyle that can contribute to recovery from CFS. The chapters that follow are intended to help you follow through with healthful changes.

This discussion should not be construed as suggesting that CFS is a disease of lifestyle. Far from it, for we have already discussed the multicausal perspective. However, just as any disease process is multicausal, so too is recovery. The way various factors combine to allow disease does not necessarily dictate what factors will promote recovery. In other words, even if genetic vulnerability played a larger than usual role in one person's developing CFS, this does not mean that lifestyle factors cannot be the key in swinging the body's balance back in the direction of health.

* * *

Experience with what were formerly thought of as irreversible illnesses such as metastatic cancers, AIDS, and heart disease has proven that profound lifestyle changes can cause dramatic changes in the course of illness. In some cases people have been able to completely break the textbook rules of disease and arrive at previously unheard of recoveries. An example of this is Niro, a documented case of AIDS who recovered and converted back to HIV negative. Another is Larry, who recovered from metastatic pancreatic cancer, even though his doctors agreed that what little chemotherapy he was taking could not possibly have made any difference.

In the medical world, these are usually labeled "spontaneous recovery," implying that since the recovery could not be attributed to medical treatment, it must have happened all by itself as a random fluke of nature. It certainly could not have anything to do with the *person* with the illness!

Dr. Kenneth Pelletier of the University of California's San Francisco Medical School studied the common denominators in people sharing the experience of such unexplained recovery. He found the following qualities often to be present:

(1) profound intrapsychic change through meditation, prayer, or other spiritual practice;
(2) profound interpersonal changes as a result, placing relations with other people on a more solid footing;
(3) alterations in diet, no longer taking food for granted, but choosing food carefully for optimum nutrition;
(4) a deep sense of the spiritual as well as material aspects of life; and
(5) a feeling that recovery is not a gift or spontaneous remission, but rather a long, hard struggle to be won for oneself.[2]

What can people with CFS learn from this? Clearly these are all factors that involve lifestyle change. Research has shown that these changes have their beneficial effects by altering the chemical and emotional environment within the body, thereby affecting the immune system. A lifestyle which has such beneficial effects may be called "salutogenic," in which "saluto" means health and "genic" means to generate or create. This is the opposite of "pathogenic," or generating pathology.

Tina's story offers us an example of what it means to make the transition to a salutogenic lifestyle:

"I quit my job, got the stress out of my life, got into therapy and started becoming aware of myself and how I live. Fortunately, I could take a job as a consultant, and only had to work part-time to make the same salary I made before. I'm not sure I could ever work full-time again, unless it was something I loved so much it didn't matter. I now actually enjoy the company I work for. I no longer put myself in a position of getting so stressed out that I am likely to relapse."

Let us now consider several aspects of a salutogenic lifestyle I have found important for people living with CFS.

Optimism and Belief in Recovery

Do you believe recovery is possible for you? Do you believe you can have some impact on it? And can you picture yourself recovered? Belief in recovery is square one. Whether it is recovering your pre-illness level of functioning, which many have done; recovering the quality of your life; or recovering a sense of balance and harmony even within limitations, there needs to be some positive expectancy that your life can be better than it is now.

There is mounting evidence that optimism has an effect on recovery from chronic illness. For example, studies by Michael Scheier, Ph.D., and his colleagues at Carnegie-Mellon University in Pittsburgh have found faster recovery in optimistic patients with cancer and heart disease than in those who are pessimistic, findings that are likely to apply to people with other illnesses as well.[3] Optimistic patients recovered faster from surgery, had fewer complications, and had higher quality of life six months later. The researchers found that when patients are optimistic, they formulate plans for action, and stay with them through pain and adversity.

How can you strengthen your optimistic attitude? Give yourself a quiet time to form an image of what recovery truly means to you. Considering what you have learned about CFS and the experiences of former CFS sufferers, make a realistic appraisal of the severity of your illness, your strengths and inner resources, and then decide for yourself where you are headed with your recovery program. You may wish to have stepping stones along the way, small goals within reasonably easy reach, to encourage you along. But the belief must be there that life can be better, and that recovery of something you value is possible for you.

Without belief in recovery, in whatever form, there will be no incentive to follow through with the lifestyle changes needed. This inner image of your recovery must be in place.

Accepting Your Limitations

One of the most difficult yet important challenges in CFS, as with any chronic illness, is accepting limitations. The fact is you are not the same person you were before, and we have already mentioned the importance of acknowledging this. Consider Sarah's experience:

"I haven't pushed my limits. Before I got CFS, I was running twelve to fifteen miles every day, training for half-marathons and marathons. Even though I'm over it, I don't do that anymore. I don't run more than six miles at any given time now for this specific reason: I'm no longer interested in testing my limits or competing. I've done it all, it's behind me. I learned that the hard way. That's an important point to put across because there are so many CFS patients who were athletic, who did push their limits, who are compulsive, high-energy, goal-directed people. They have to learn a new way."

Often the acceptance of limitations means a shift of identity away from your outward accomplishments, your "doing," as the indication of who you are and whether you are fully alive. This cultural emphasis on "doing" is deeply ingrained in us. It comes into direct conflict with the body's messages in CFS, that rest, or "simply being," is needed for healing.

When the desires of the mind and the abilities of the body have parted company, our tendency is to resist, to argue with the body. We may take the attitude that limitations are a challenge or test, or, worse yet, a sign of defeat. Yet, to reiterate what has been said earlier, the more we attempt to push through limitations, the more we are likely to cause an exacerbation of symptoms or trigger relapse.

Accepting limitations in some cases may mean stepping out of your familiar roles at home, designating traditional responsibilities to others. For many people a dramatic reduction in working hours is necessary. In more extreme cases, it means stopping work altogether. To the degree that your work is your source of identity and meaning in life, this can be painful. And, of course, the financial hardships this may bring may be even more painful. Yet, the fact remains that in order for the body to have the optimal conditions for healing, rest is needed. Not only for the body, but for the mind as well.

There are several stresses at play here. One is the stress of the illness itself. Another is the stress of work, which you may not necessarily think of as a negative stress, but still, to the degree that it involves challenge and any demands at all, the body may experience it as stress. And third is the stress created by your reaction to the limitations being forced upon you. To take a philosophical attitude or somehow accept and flow with these limitations will go a long way toward supporting your healing process. This, of course, is where the fifty-percent solution takes on even greater significance because of its consequences. Working fewer hours than you feel capable may be an especially hard choice because of economic concerns, but these have to be weighed against the long-term costs of not getting well.

If reducing your work is forcing a reduction in your income, it may mean making major changes in your living arrangements. In a worst case scenario, this may mean moving to less costly accommodations or even living temporarily with relatives or friends. Some would perceive this as a demoralizing situation, yet it may be the only viable alternative to struggling and stressing yourself to work more than you are able and interfering with your healing process. Again, your reactions to the limitations imposed on you can help you or can themselves be an added source of debilitating stress. Accepting such limitations gracefully can be difficult, but it can be done.

The Value of Supportive Relationships

One of the fascinating areas of research in health psychology in recent years has been the effect of relationships on health. It is now believed that supportive relationships help "buffer" the person from the effects of stress. Some researchers even call social support a form of inoculation against illness.

What is a supportive relationship? This would probably be answered differently by different people. But there are some basic attributes on which most would agree. One of these is open communication. This means honest sharing of feelings, wants, needs, and caring. It also means that the parties feel free to say "no" when they wish, without feeling guilty. In this environment of mutual respect, there is freedom to be oneself without fear of judgment. There is a feeling of acceptance, and an encouragement of self-acceptance on both sides.

On the other hand, relationships in which there is an undercurrent of tension, fear, or inability to freely be oneself may be described as toxic relationships. They can literally have a toxic effect on the body, in terms of the chemistry of stress that they stimulate.

People with CFS benefit from supportive relationships in several ways. Mood and morale are likely to be better. Follow-through with lifestyle changes and medical treatment are likely to be better because of the encouragement and support of others to do so.

Coping with stress may be more effective because of guidance or encouragement from others. Feelings of having purpose or meaning in life may be stronger, and contribute to greater will to live and hope for recovery. All these factors can translate into better immune functioning and resistance against illness.

The people closest to you can play an important role in your healing. They can contribute the healing, supportive environment which you need. They can give you love, encouragement, and help in carrying out the various lifestyle changes you need to make. They can help you with practical matters such as getting to medical treatment, shopping, or completing tasks around your home. They can help you follow the 50 percent solution, accept your limitations and encourage you as you walk the path of self-empowerment.

However, none of these forms of support will be forthcoming unless you communicate your needs. The key to social support, as in all human relationships, is communication. Those around you are going to need *your* help understanding what CFS is, as well as what forms of support you need.

Some people with CFS are lucky enough to have a supportive network already in place. However, others are not so lucky and must orchestrate the support they need. If this is the case for you, one of the best ways to do this is for you or a loved one to call a gathering to communicate about your situation. Whether it is a potluck dinner, a family meeting, or a larger gathering with friends or co-workers, this can be a very effective way of organizing support.

Symbolically, such a gathering sends a powerful statement to all those involved: we are part of a larger whole, a tribe, we are connected. Even though such an idea may sound bold, if you give it a try you are most likely in for a pleasant surprise. This is actually a tradition thousands of years old in simpler societies.

Families face special difficulties as a result of CFS, since illness in one family member affects the entire family system. The family meeting, in which all members are able to express their feelings and needs, is very helpful. Such a meeting can be set up so that everyone has a turn in talking about what is important for them, and can ask questions. Many families have a regular evening each week specifically devoted to this kind of communication.

Very often, marriage and family counseling sessions can help enormously in maintaining lines of communication. Whether such counseling is with a psychologist, clinical social worker, counselor, minister, or a member of your medical team, communication will be the key. Communication itself has a healing effect on relationships that are hurting. Many CFS patients have reported their families have grown closer and have benefited from facing the adversity of CFS together.

The experience of giving to another in need brings its own rewards. By accepting support from others, you give them an opportunity to feel valued and included in your life. This is a form of intimacy that we all need in an age where separateness and independence are over-emphasized. Many people with CFS have been profoundly moved by the unexpected degree of care and support they have received. However, you have to be open to asking for and receiving the support you need.

Supporting Yourself

Do you consider yourself a person with high self-esteem? Can you find feelings of love, compassion, and unconditional acceptance toward yourself? If so, then you will have an easier time following through with healthful lifestyle changes, and in general coping with CFS. But if there is an inner climate of self-criticism, self-judgment, or guilt, then the kind of inner support you need is not likely to be present.

Many of us have lived lifestyles in which low self-esteem, high self-criticism, and a never-ending quest for the approval of others have dominated our behavior. If this is the case for you, CFS can serve to force you to re-evaluate your relationship with yourself, and make a shift toward valuing or esteeming yourself more highly.

One way this positive shift can be expressed is in how you spend your time. Do you surrender your life to the television? Do you occupy your time reading romance novels, or perhaps worse, CFS research?

Quality alone time is time in which you are fully *present* with yourself rather than being absorbed by something outside yourself. This kind of presence is not only a natural antidote to the effects of stress, it will help you remember who you are, to remain in touch with your needs as well as your higher goals and purposes, and remain intimately aware of the ebbing and flowing of your body's cycles.

Rarely in our society are we encouraged to spend quality time alone. This can be time spent in meditation, prayer, journal writing, or contemplating nature. Perhaps you choose to pursue a self-healing discipline, such as deep breathing, deep relaxation, guided imagery, gentle yoga, or a number of other practices. Or it may simply mean sitting quietly doing nothing, watching the grass grow, and letting both mind and body rest.

PLEASURE AND ENJOYMENT

Even if it means settling for pleasures much simpler than those you became accustomed to before becoming ill, find ways to include pleasure and enjoyment in your daily life. Whether it comes in the form of physical touch or contact with another, watering flowers, cultivating your taste in music, or becoming a connoisseur of bath oils, you can develop your own repertoire of simple pleasures.

Keeping pleasure in your life sends a powerful message to your subconscious—one which supports your self-esteem and feelings of worthiness, and helps maintain your morale. But this contribution to your inner harmony and balance is only half the benefit. Pleasure also causes beneficial changes in your blood chemistry, which help your body's healing responses.

The health benefits of pleasure have been studied by David Sobel, M.D., M.P.H.[4] Dr. Sobel is Regional Director of Patient Education and Health Promotion for Kaiser Permanente Medical Care Program of Northern California. He points out that our affinity for pleasure played a major role in our evolution as a species. The experience of genuine pleasure alters our biochemistry in a way that promotes our host resistance. Hence there are real links between health-promoting acts, positive feelings, and health.

The simple pleasures listed can all have a calming and relaxing effect on the body, soothing body and soul from the effects of stress. However, as Dr. Sobel emphasizes, pleasure is not limited to experiences of the senses. Acts of generosity, altruism, and gratitude also are pleasurable and bring about beneficial responses in your body. He concludes that these acts represent not only moral virtues; they may be essential contributors to a longer, healthier life.[5]

However ill you are, you can probably find a way to experience selfless giving and reap the health benefits of altruism. Simple acts of kindness or consideration can be done with people around you, as well as with pets or plants. You will be doing your body a wonderful favor.

SPIRITUALITY

As the experience of illness draws your attention more and more within yourself, you may find yourself increasingly interested in the spiritual aspects of your life. And indeed, there are questions which science and medicine cannot answer which are more the domain of the spiritual.

Why do I have this illness? Is there any meaning in it? For many, the crisis of CFS has provoked profound spiritual searching and introspection. This in turn has borne fruit in the form of a greater sense that we are more than either our bodies or our minds, and that there are sources of support and energy within that can help us get through the hardest times. Whether you explore your spiritual life through a form of organized religion, on your own, or with friends or loved ones, there is a good chance this will contribute to the quality of your life.

In addition, there is now evidence that physical health is influenced in a positive way by religious faith. David Larson, M.D., a psychiatrist with the National Institute of Mental Health, recently reported a twenty-year study in which people's belief in the importance of religion was linked to healthier blood-pressure levels.[6] In another study, Larson found that older, religious women recovered more quickly from broken hips and with less depression than their non-religious counterparts.[7]

A related line of research connects religious faith and mental health. Here, too, there is mounting evidence of benefit. In a review of two hundred studies, a team of Maryland researchers concluded that religious faith eases depression and is linked to better recovery from mental illness.[8] It is not difficult to see that people with CFS will benefit from anything that eases or buffers the emotional stress of the illness. Indeed, several patients have told me that their faith has strengthened through this ordeal. According to Mike, "I've been pretty religious all my life, but through CFS I think my prayers had more depth and intensity, and more thought went into them than before."

This illness may provoke you to reconsider your life goals and purposes. What is your purpose for getting well? Is it simply to resume being a productive worker? Is it to resume the pleasures you are currently being denied? Or are you becoming aware of higher goals and more important dimensions of your life that give it real meaning? Are you living according to your deeper values? Many people with CFS find that the purpose or meaning of their life shifts, that their values change, and that the changes brought by illness have enriched their lives. We'll discuss these potential outgrowths of CFS in the last chapter.

Basic Nutrition

Understanding the role of nutrition in health is not one of modern medicine's strengths. Our fascination with pharmaceuticals, microbes, and high-tech medicine has diverted our attention away from simpler, more fundamental factors that influence our health on a moment to moment basis. Yet food and nutrition directly and continuously influence the body's resistance to illness.

There are common substances in the normal Western diet that are now known to weaken immunity, and should be especially avoided by people with immune-related illnesses. These include refined sugar, caffeine, alcohol, and many kinds of food additives. Other substances are known to be the raw materials of the immune system, actually used in building white cells. Such substances include many vitamins and minerals, especially vitamin C and zinc.

It is easy to become overwhelmed by the mountain of information and claims about various nutrients and immunity. Rather than having to be a research scientist to eat intelligently, there are some broad guidelines which should help you arrive at a reasonably healthy nutritional program.

A WHOLE-FOODS DIET
Our bodies evolved throughout history on a diet very different from that which we eat today. We would spend a fortune in health-food stores to eat the way our ancestors did. They lived on what we would call a "special diet," one of natural, organic, whole, unprocessed foods. Their fruits and vegetables were only fresh and in season, in their natural state, free of chemical residues. They ate meat, eggs, and poultry that were uncompromised by growth stimulants, antibiotics, or preservatives. They ate fresh fish from unpolluted waterways and oceans. They drank water untainted by agricultural or industrial chemicals. Their immune sys-

tems were not burdened with the toxic by-products of modern chemistry.

The concept of a whole-foods diet is central in a salutogenic lifestyle. This means unprocessed foods, whole grains, untainted with preservatives or additives, and ideally, if available, organically grown fruits and vegetables. Unchemicalized poultry, eggs, and meat can be purchased in many areas (without growth hormones or antibiotics). Freshwater fish should be avoided because of pollution by industrial or agricultural chemicals. Likewise, shellfish tend to collect toxins and should also be avoided. A good rule of thumb is to read the ingredients on packaged foods. The fewer ingredients, the better. And if there is anything you cannot easily pronounce, don't buy it!

DRINKING WATER

Pure drinking water is increasingly hard to come by. Yet the body is mostly water, and uses water to dissolve toxins and cleanse its tissues. As we have already seen, the activity of the immune system in CFS produces many toxic by-products which must be dissolved and released from the body. The more pure water is, the more "aggressive" or effective it is in dissolving impurities and toxins. Hence, drinking purified water is an important contribution to a healing environment in the body.

There are several kinds of water purifiers available, and using any one of them is probably an improvement over drinking tap water. Two major types of purifiers are carbon filters and reverse osmosis. While reverse osmosis is slower and more expensive, it is generally more effective in filtering out impurities. The best purifiers have both carbon filtration and a reverse osmosis membrane working together, but again, anything is likely to be better than nothing. Most filters are accompanied by lab test results which, if you feel you can trust them, give a way of comparing the effectiveness of filters.

An alternative is to purchase bottled water. The drawback to this is that you may not know the quality of the water, or what method of purification was used. It is possible that so-called "natural spring water" can have high levels of impurities even though it is packaged beautifully. And, of course, not all impurities are man-made. Water coming from natural sources can be contaminated with toxic levels of substances occurring naturally in the environment. Thus, the safest course is usually to have your own purification process.

Nutritional Supplementation

"Hypovitaminosis" is thought by some physicians to be an important feature of CFS. This refers to vitamin deficiency at the cellular level, which may not be reflected in conventional tests of vitamin levels in the blood. According to Paul Cheney, M.D., the elevated cytokine levels in CFS can block the vitamin utilization pathways in immune cells, producing a "hypovitaminosis syndrome" which further impairs immune functioning.[9] For this reason, Dr. Cheney recommends multivitamin therapy for CFS patients.

This gives us even more reason to consider supplementation as an important part of your recovery plan. Your immune system is already working overtime and depleting its resources by being in a state of hyper-arousal. In order for it to heal it needs the energy and raw materials that can only be provided through nutrients.

One physician who integrates a nutritional approach into treatment of CFS is Murray Susser, M.D., who states: "The body is designed for aboriginal eating. So if you're not eating beetles and worms and grubs and the like, then you're not going to be healthy no matter how smart you are about nutrition—unless you find the right supplements to make up for that lack."[10]

According to Dr. Susser, "functional" vitamin tests can be used to determine to what degree your cells are actually using the vitamins you take in. Such tests are not yet widely available in mainstream medicine, but, along with therapeutic trials, have revealed a great deal of hypovitaminosis in CFS patients.

An abundance of research has shown that certain vitamins are important in healthy immune functioning. These include vitamins A (retinol), B_1 (thiamin), B_2 (riboflavin), B_6 (pyridoxine), B_{12} (cyanocobalamin), folic acid, pantothenic acid, C (ascorbic acid), D, and E. Minerals affecting immunity include copper, iron, magnesium, manganese, selenium, and zinc. There are also essential amino acids and essential fatty acids that play a role in immunity. An excellent summary of research on nutrition and immunity is offered in *Nutritional Influences on Illness,* by Melvyn Werbach, M.D. (Third Line Press, Tarzana, California, 1987). This kind of information is widely available now, and there are many other books that could be recommended in popular bookstores.

WHAT SHOULD I TAKE, AND HOW MUCH?

Most people are best advised to get individualized help in answering this question. Vitamin and mineral supplementation should be guided by a knowledgeable health professional, either a qualified nutritionist or a physician. Proper amounts must be taken, because *both deficiencies and over-supplementation* of some nutrients can adversely affect immunity. Also, some nutrients need to be taken in combination with others (zinc with copper, for example). Do not rely on the RDA (recommended dietary allowances) for guidance. These were never intended as therapeutic guidelines, but rather were designed for minimal nutritional requirements of mass populations during World War II.

THE ABSORPTION ISSUE

One important issue in supplementation is that of absorption. Supplements taken by mouth are of course not as well absorbed as those taken by injection. In fact, many CFS patients have benefited from vitamin B_{12} injections. However, since oral administration is most common, it is important to know that certain forms are better than others.

Tablets which have been pressed together are less well absorbed than encapsulated crystallized vitamins. The hard tablets are often heated to a temperature far above where the vitamins can maintain their effectiveness. Vitamins B and C, for example, lose their potency at 180 degrees, but in tabulation machines often reach temperatures of 400 degrees.

MAINTAINING COLON HEALTH

Finally, supplementation can be a means of maintaining colon health. As discussed earlier, yeast overgrowth in the colon and in the rest of the body is a common problem in people with CFS which contributes to immune dysfunction, allergies, food sensitivities, and immune overactivation. Yeast problems often develop when antibiotic therapy kills the healthful bacteria that populate the colon. Further, the standard American diet (the "S.A.D.") promotes yeast overgrowth with its refined sugar and highly processed foods.

As Carol Jessop, M.D., states: "I think that there is a lot of strong information to suggest that (CFS) patients have yeast overgrowth or parasitic intestinal overgrowth. In my clinical experience, when I document yeast and prescribe treatment, the patient's immune system seems somewhat less activated, and therefore, may be better able to deal with the agent or agents that are causing this syndrome . . . I think that this is one of the reasons my patients improve over a period of time."[11]

The first line of defense against yeast overgrowth is a diet high in complex carbohydrates (such as whole foods, whole grains), and low in simple carbohydrates (such as sugar, white flour, refined products). There are many good books available on anti-yeast diets and recipes. Essentially, a whole-foods diet with minimal refined products or simple sugars will help prevent yeast overgrowth.

During and after any treatment with antibiotic drugs, it is important to restore a balance of healthful bacteria in the colon, which is essential for good digestion and prevention of yeast overgrowth. This can be done by supplementation with a variety of forms of acidophilus and other healthful bacteria, available in powder or liquid form. Unless the form of supplementation is of a type which is unaffected by stomach acid, it needs to be taken on an empty stomach (usually first thing in the morning) so it is not destroyed on its way to the colon.

There are also supplements such as odorless garlic tablets, Mycocidin, and ParaMicrocidin which help fight yeast overgrowth. Holistically oriented physicians are usually well-informed about the issues of yeast treatment.

Yeast overgrowth is best diagnosed by purged stool testing and blood testing, and may need to be treated with antifungal drugs. According to Dr. Jessop, the great majority of patients with CFS are not tested using purged stool samples and are not correctly evaluated for this condition. There are effective antifungals available now, and as Jessop reports, such treatment gets into the nervous system and results in improvement in the symptoms of cognitive dysfunction affecting many people with CFS.

Changing Your Physical Environment

Changing the physical environment around you can have a surprising effect on your moods and inner states. Plants or flowers, cleanliness and neatness, clean windows, repositioning furniture, and lighting are all subtle changes that can create a more emotionally comfortable environment. When you make such changes, the mere action of doing so makes a statement about taking charge and valuing yourself.

Beyond the aesthetics, however, is an even more important issue of avoiding toxic materials in your environment. In Chapter 5 we discussed how the environment is involved in sensitivities and sensory dysfunction in CFS. To reiterate, cleaning materials in particular are offenders in terms of exposing you to immunosuppressing toxins. Given your state of vulnerability, it is best to use only natural and nontoxic cleaning materials.

Other possible offenders include the glue in carpeting. Especially avoid new carpeting unless it is clearly marked as natural and nontoxic. Also problematic are toxins and fumes escaping from paint and new building materials, such as the glue and formaldehyde in plywood. In fact, in many cases of CFS, encounters with toxic substances appear to have played a significant role. Make sure those around you are also aware of materials which are harmful for you.

Very often creating the environment you need requires standing up for your needs, as Marge tells us: "My contractor installed this fiberboard in the attic that released terrible glue fumes. I just decided I wouldn't accept it, and I didn't have to understand the chemistry or justify it in order to tell him to remove it. At first I did a real number on myself about 'inconveniencing' him, but I decided, after all, it was my house. So I asked him to return it and just use wood."

* * *

It's certainly worth repeating that lifestyle change *can* provide the major impetus to recovery. As we have seen, there is a great deal you can do to create a lifestyle that will support you. I have suggested a lot of changes here. However, there is no need to feel overwhelmed and think that you have to do everything according to this or any other book. Beware of any voices in the head saying you have to "do it right!" And, fortunately, with the growing recognition of CFS in the health community, you do not have to do it alone. In the next chapter we will explore the variety of psychosocial support services available to help you make the changes you wish, and make them last.

Following are two exercises to help you take stock of your current lifestyle and identify what you might need to change.

EXERCISE 1: ASSESSING YOUR LIFESTYLE
The exercise below is offered as a review and summary of major points to consider in evaluating your own lifestyle. All of the items listed affect your ability to resist illness. Take plenty of time to consider each answer, and go deeper than your first impressions.

Instructions: Place one of the following symbols beside each item, signifying how well you feel you are doing with that item:
+ means you are doing well with this
o means you are doing "so-so" and could improve
− means you definitely need to improve with this

1. NUTRITION:
___ A. I drink purified water.
___ B. I drink *enough* purified water (six to eight glasses a day).
___ C. I eat breakfast.
___ D. I eat on a regular schedule.
___ E. I am careful to avoid processed foods.
___ F. I eat fresh fruits and vegetables.
___ G. I take appropriate supplementation.
___ H. I avoid refined sugar.
___ I. I minimize red meat intake.
___ J. I avoid alcohol.

___ K. I avoid caffeine.
___ L. I read the labels on food packages.
___ M. I avoid foods with chemicals I can't pronounce.

2. ENVIRONMENT:

___ A. I keep my environment free of toxic chemicals and fumes, including cigarette smoke.
___ B. I keep my environment relatively quiet and peaceful.
___ C. I keep my environment beautiful and uplifting.

3. RELATIONSHIPS:

___ A. I communicate my feelings clearly.
___ B. I communicate my wants and needs clearly.
___ C. I say "no" without feeling guilty.
___ D. I am free from unresolved, festering conflicts.
___ E. I am free from preoccupation with old hurts.
___ F. I avoid "toxic relationships."
___ G. I have relationships which nourish me.

4. EMOTIONAL EXPRESSION:

___ A. I allow and express sadness.
___ B. I cry freely.
___ C. I allow and express fear.
___ D. I allow and express anger.
___ E. I allow and express love.
___ F. I allow and express joy.
___ G. I laugh freely.

5. SELF-ESTEEM:

___ A. I am free of guilt and self-judgment.
___ B. I forgive myself for past mistakes.
___ C. I love and accept myself.

6. ALONE TIME:

___ A. I spend some quality time alone each day.
___ B. I let my mind rest.
___ C. I relax.
___ D. I spend time in introspection.

7. ACTIVITY:

___ A. I get mild, comfortable exercise when I feel able.

___ B. My work activity is free of anxiety and compulsiveness.

___ C. My home-making activity is free of anxiety and compulsiveness.

___ D. I allow myself to rest when I need to.

8. PLEASURE AND ENJOYMENT:

___ A. I get some genuine pleasure or enjoyment each day.

___ B. I initiate contact with friends I enjoy.

9. PHYSICAL TOUCH AND CONTACT WITH OTHERS:

___ A. I have physical contact with others.

___ B. I give and receive affection.

___ C. I accept affection gracefully without having to talk about it or having to give something back right away.

10. THE SPIRITUAL DIMENSION OF LIFE:

___ A. I have a spiritual or religious understanding for my life which assists me to feel peaceful, hopeful, and at ease with my life.

___ B. I have personal goals which make my life worthwhile.

___ C. I have a deep, valuable purpose for being well.

___ D. I truly believe in my purpose for being well.

___ E. I am living life according to my deeper values.

11. SELF-HELP:

___ A. I actively seek information about my health on my own.

___ B. I ask my doctor questions and keep asking until I am satisfied.

___ C. I practice some form of self-help activity each day.

EXERCISE 2: IMAGINING A HEALTHY LIFESTYLE

Develop an image of what would be the optimal lifestyle to promote your healing. Include all the areas discussed in this chapter and anything else you feel would be important. Especially include seeing yourself doing what would be most fulfilling and inspiring to you.

It may be helpful to write down a description in first person, present tense, of how you are living in this healthy lifestyle. Let this image become something you contemplate regularly, and gradually it will begin to influence your lifestyle choices day by day.

7

The Benefits of Mind/Body Medicine

"The imagery and relaxation training have helped me more than any medication. I can actually feel physical changes in my body. That takes away the anxiety I feel with this illness."   —Alice

In 1987, Alice participated in my self-help program in Incline Village, Nevada. At the time she was undergoing a two-week intensive treatment of intravenous Acyclovir therapy in the hospital. Acyclovir is a drug which inhibits the reproduction of viruses of the herpes family, to which HHV6 and Epstein-Barr virus belong. One of the side effects of acyclovir therapy is escalating blood pressure, which needs to be closely monitored.

Alice was about halfway through her treatment protocol when she enrolled in the group. She brought her stainless-steel drip apparatus with her from the hospital, and stood it up beside her in the circle with the other patients and their spouses.

The first day involved a series of relaxation and deep breathing exercises. The next day Alice returned to the group, bubbling with excitement. She reported that the previous evening her blood pressure had returned to normal. The nursing staff were mystified, and wanted to know how she had done it.

The benefits Alice received are not at all uncommon. They illustrate the fact that we can directly influence what goes on in our body. The branch of medicine that uses behavior change for influencing the physical body is called behavioral medicine, or more popularly, mind/body medicine. In recent years mind/body medicine has been increasingly finding its way into the mainstream. In chronic illnesses like CFS, HIV, cancer, it lies at the heart of self-empowerment. In this chapter we will examine the benefits—and some unexpected problems—that can arise in using mind/body medicine in CFS.

Perhaps this is a good time to reiterate the fact that CFS is not a psychosomatic disease. "Psychosomatic" means the mind is the root cause of symptoms in the body. If anything, CFS is a "somato-psychic" disease. The events in the body—specifically the immune system—influence the brain, mind, and emotions. In mind/body medicine, however, we are deliberately using the pathways of connection between mind and body to influence what goes on in the body. In a sense we are exploiting the mind/body connections to make things happen in our favor.

The person with CFS is likely to encounter several different forms of psychological services, and mind/body techniques may be a part of any of them. Possible forms of psychological help include individual or family therapy, group therapy, hypnotherapy and medical hypnosis—and several derivatives of these.

Because they are used to help with a physical illness, these are all forms of "complementary therapy."[1] This means they work alongside medical treatment in a supportive way. I like this term because it communicates its relationship with medical treatment—that it does not replace or compete with it, but acts in partnership with it. This is an important distinction because many people erroneously think of mind/body medicine as "alternative" medicine, something which you would use *instead of* medical treatment. No responsible health professional would recommend these approaches as alternatives to established treatment.

In this chapter we will survey the range of psychological therapies that can be used to promote recovery from CFS. This includes individual and group therapies, as well as mind/body medicine techniques you can use on your own. This will lay the groundwork for the "how to" chapters that follow, dealing with specific techniques.

What Kinds of Psychological Help
Are Available for CFS?

Very little research has been done to study the benefits of psychological therapies with CFS. However, we can borrow insights from
work with other immune-related illnesses to gauge the role and
likely benefits of such intervention in CFS. Below we will consider
the benefits of the various approaches you are most likely to encounter.

PSYCHOTHERAPY

Psychotherapy is conducted by a trained, licensed or certified therapist (clinical psychologist, clinical social worker, marriage and family therapist, or psychiatrist). Of course, before entering into such a
relationship with a therapist, you should determine whether they
are informed about CFS. Many are not, and may be inclined to take
a "psychosomatic" orientation toward this condition. Always make
sure they have done their homework.

Psychotherapy offers an excellent opportunity to explore your
feelings about your situation, identify problems in relating with your
family, learn how to manage symptoms, or explore the challenges
in coping with chronic illness. Though such therapy may be brief,
it can have important benefits. One of the greatest benefits is improving the quality of life.

As discussed earlier, the challenges of CFS require a great deal of
coping, not only with the symptoms but with the stress of illness in
general. Therapy can be very helpful in reminding you to respect
your limits, that symptoms are transitory, that healing is possible,
and to follow through with self-help practices. By keeping all these
challenges in perspective, the quality of your day-to-day living can
be much improved over living in a state of constant despair or fear.

Aside from improving the quality of life, can psychotherapy influence the course of CFS? There are no definitive studies that
answer this question, although a great deal of clinical experience
strongly suggests this. And when you consider the importance of
lifestyle change and reduced stress in promoting recovery, obviously therapy can, if it helps with these issues, contribute to faster

recovery. On this point we may borrow from the cancer literature, which seems directly relevant to this issue in CFS. The value of psychotherapy is articulated by psychologist Dr. Alastair Cunningham, who states:

> Although epidemiological considerations suggest that the contribution of psychological factors to cancer onset is small . . . compared to purely biological and social factors (e.g., environmental carcinogens), no upper limit to what can be achieved by psychotherapy is necessarily thereby set: the relative influence of the psyche on outcome may be greatly expanded by such therapy, overriding the usual progression of disease.[2]

There are certain risks in placing a great deal of emphasis on psychotherapy for physical healing, however. These will be discussed at length later in this chapter.

GROUP PROGRAMS

There is no question that group participation can be valuable. A group can be a source of inspiration, emotional support, and information about handling symptoms. Two basic kinds of groups are available: support groups led by peers, and group programs led by professionally trained therapists.

Support Groups

These groups offer an especially good arena for exchanging information about physicians, treatment, and research news. Support groups are also helpful in overcoming the isolation and lack of social support which so many people with CFS experience. And they can be a source of reinforcement for continuing on your path of self-empowerment.

You can gain a great deal from witnessing how others handle the challenge of illness, and in what ways their journey might parallel your own. The support group can also be a rich resource of wisdom and experience in devising coping strategies for symptoms and for the emotional distress of illness.

There is a downside to support groups. You are not likely to meet people who have recovered in such a group, leaving the impression that no one recovers. Also some groups can inadvertently reinforce the "victim" role. That is, they can become a place where your identity as a "victim of CFS" is actually strengthened, and this can subtly work against your sense of hope and positive expectancy about recovery. The risks of this happening are especially high in those few groups where the emphasis seems to be on exchanging horror stories about symptoms.

I have heard many patients say they have chosen to quit attending support groups because of this problem of dwelling on the negative. Yet there are times, especially early in the illness, when it is a relief to know that you are not alone in your experience of your symptoms.

You must judge for yourself whether a particular support group has its focus in the right place for you. Is it reinforcing self-empowerment? This is a good question to discuss with the other participants.

You can determine whether there is a CFS support group in your area by contacting the resources listed in Appendix D.

Group Therapy Programs

These groups are usually led by credentialed, professional therapists, and are generally organized around teaching specific skills such as relaxation, meditation, imagery, pain control, stress reduction, and coping with the stress of illness.

Many such groups have been studied and found to have positive impact, not only on quality of life, but in some cases on immune functioning and health status.

One example is the Self-Help Intensive at the Cancer Support and Education Center, Menlo Park, California.[3] While originally designed for cancer patients, the program also serves people with CFS and other chronic illnesses. The ten-day, sixty-hour program helps people with imagery and relaxation training, lifestyle change, emotional expression, strengthening fighting spirit, and using their illness as a teacher.

I conducted an outcome study of this program as part of my doctoral dissertation at the University of California at Berkeley, before joining the staff of the Center. The study involved fifty-nine cancer patients who took the Self-Help Intensive, and found significant improvements in emotional expression, fighting spirit, and several aspects of quality of life. It also showed that people in even the more advanced stages of illness can benefit from such training.[4] The benefits were still present three months after completing the program, indicating that the effects can be lasting.

A similar study of forty-eight patients with HIV who also took the same Self-Help Intensive found significant improvement in emotional expression and health locus of control, and reduced tension, anxiety, fatigue, depression, and total mood disturbance.[5] These findings, as well as those of the cancer patient study, represent improvements that have been found in the more general PNI research to be associated with better immune functioning.

At UCLA, a team of researchers studied outcomes of a group program for sixty-six post-surgical malignant melanoma patients.[6] The six-week structured group program included health education, stress management, training in problem-solving, and psychological support. Results showed significant improvement in both psychological coping and immune functioning. Six months after the program, there were significantly lower levels of psychological distress, and higher levels of positive coping methods in comparison to patients who did not have the group. *There were also significant increases in the percentage of NK cells and in NK cell cytotoxic activity (their functional effectiveness).*

One of the more exciting studies in this field dealt with increasing survival time in cancer. David Spiegel, M.D., and his colleagues at Stanford University and UC Berkeley conducted a ten-year study of eighty-six women with metastatic breast cancer.[7] The groups lasted a year, meeting weekly for ninety minutes, and used a form of therapy called "supportive-expressive therapy." Though the researchers had set out to study quality of life, they were surprised to find that survival time was nearly double that of a comparable group of women not receiving the group therapy (averaging thirty-six months versus eighteen months).

This highly regarded study represents a breakthrough in linking psychological treatment with medical outcome. How could the difference in survival time have occurred? We do not know whether the benefit was due to a particular technique of therapy, the experience of belonging or affiliation in the group, emotional expression, shifts in attitude, improved compliance with medical recommendations, or changes in other lifestyle behaviors that were encouraged by the group.

It is also possible that, since the immune system is the main line of defense in cancer, the results were due to improved immune responses alone. Or, perhaps most likely, the results were multicausal, and many different impacts of the program had a synergistic effect. These questions are now being pursued by Spiegel and his research team. Meanwhile, as a result of this study, group therapy is now being seen in a different light compared to before when it was thought of as only a quality of life intervention.

The effects reported in the above studies represent a growing body of findings about benefits of group programs for people with immune-related illnesses. I consider it highly likely that when similar studies are conducted for people with CFS, we will find similar benefits. In the meantime, I encourage you to seek out group therapy programs—taking care, of course, to be sure that whoever is leading the program has an accurate understanding of CFS.

Mind/Body Medicine

The term "mind/body medicine" covers a variety of techniques you can use to help the mind influence the body. The basic tools of mind/body medicine include relaxation training, meditation, imagery, and related approaches. These are frequently used in the group and individual therapy programs discussed above.

Later chapters will be devoted to showing you how to use these methods with CFS. But first, I would like to acquaint you with the rationale, and especially the research backing, for the use of these techniques.

Mind/body medicine is usually thought of as something new, controversial, subject to abuse or false claims, and needing a lot of study to prove that it has any value. However, the principles of mind/body medicine are actually among the most thoroughly tested in all of medical science. I can make this unusual statement because the mind/body connection is tested in virtually all research on new drugs.

Typically, when a new drug is being tested, some patients are given the drug and some are given a "placebo," a fake pill such as a useless sugar pill. The placebo triggers a positive expectancy or hope in the mind of the person taking it. Often this will result in changes in the body, called placebo effects.

The drug might then be rejected because it is found to be no better than the placebo effect. The researchers may say in disappointment, "We found nothing of value. The drug was no better than placebo." The flip side of this statement, of course, is, "We have proven once again the power of mind/body medicine. It is just as effective as the drug."

In mind/body medicine, we are deliberately exploiting the pathways used in the placebo response. The viability of these pathways has been proven by literally thousands of drug studies. Let us now turn to the techniques.

RELAXATION TRAINING

By now it should be clear that stress plays an important role in CFS. It contributes to your vulnerability to developing the syndrome, it can aggravate symptoms that are already present, and it can serve as a trigger of relapse. This all happens because stress sets off physiological and chemical changes in your body that can have toxic effects and can disturb immunity. These changes are collectively called the stress response.

Fortunately there is an antidote to the stress response. It is natural, everyone is capable of it, and it is free. It is called the relaxation response. This too is a set of physiological and chemical changes in your body. However, the changes comprising the relaxation response are opposite to the stress response—they are almost like a mirror image.

The relaxation response was discovered and named by Harvard psychiatrist Herbert Benson, M.D., and his colleagues in 1974.[8,9] They were studying a pattern of physiological changes that occurs in people practicing a form of meditation called TM (transcendental meditation). This pattern of changes was found to represent a very beneficial state, one to which meditation naturally leads. Rather than capillaries constricting and limiting the flow of blood, they open and blood flows more freely. Rather than hands and feet being cold and clammy, they are warm. Rather than heart rate increasing, it slows and relaxes. Rather than muscles being tense and tight, they become more flexible, allowing circulation to flow freely through them. Rather than breathing being rapid, shallow, and constricted, it becomes more full and deep. These are a few of the important benefits discovered by Benson and his colleagues.

We now also have evidence of its benefits for the immune system. In one study, forty-five geriatric residents were randomly assigned to one of three groups: relaxation training, social contact, and no intervention. Those in the first two groups were seen individually three times per week for a month. Blood samples were drawn before the program, immediately after the month, and a month later. Those who were trained in relaxation showed a significant improvement in NK cell activity, as well as lower antibody levels to a herpes simplex type one antigen. In addition, there were significant decreases in symptoms of emotional distress.[10]

The finding about higher NK cell functioning is especially important for CFS in that, as we have seen earlier, depressed natural killer cell activity is one of the features of this syndrome.

Further evidence of benefit to immunity comes from a study we discussed earlier, of the relationship between exam stress and immunity in thirty-four medical students. Half the students were randomly assigned to a relaxation training program. The results showed that the frequency of relaxation practice was significantly associated with the percentage of T-helper cells circulating in the blood during the exam period. In other words, the more the students practiced the relaxation response, the higher was the percentage of T-helper cells. These cells, of course, stimulate the immune response. The researchers concluded that relaxation achieved in this way may enhance at least some components of the immune system, and perhaps influence the incidence and course of disease.[11]

The regular use of the relaxation response may be one of the most healing activities we can do, yet because it's free, people tend not to value it as such. It's a simple, subtle, and powerful way of helping make room for your body's healing resources to express themselves.

IMAGERY

Imagery is a popular tool of most mind/body programs, although few scientific studies have tried to measure its effects. The use of imagery with CFS involves inventing symbols in your mind's eye which will help you play out in a visualization how you want things to occur in your body. This may involve visualizing your immune system working harmoniously and in balance; seeing your immune system eliminating viruses or other pathogens; or perhaps a general symbol to represent the syndrome, and another symbol to represent all your healing forces. In any event, visualization is a process in which you see the desired outcome develop.

How does imagery produce its effects? Scientists are investigating exactly how. It could be that the messages we are sending through the pathways connecting mind and body—the neuroimmune network discussed in Chapter 4—are heard at the cellular level, and the body respectfully responds to our commands. We could call this the "specificity hypothesis," meaning that the effects are very specific and depend on the details of the message we want to send.

There is now evidence for the specificity hypothesis. In a study at the University of Arkansas, an experienced meditator using imagery techniques was able to manipulate her immune system's reaction to an injection of harmless virus particles just below the skin. The material injected, called a "varicella zoster test reagent," ordinarily gives rise to a type of inflammation called a delayed hypersensitivity reaction. This reaction is created by white cells releasing chemicals, such as histamine, which have the effect of causing inflammation.

It was found that on demand, the woman being studied could alternately (1) suppress her inflammatory reaction and white-cell responsiveness, and (2) allow her inflammatory reaction to respond normally. This experiment suggests that she was able to communicate with and influence the behavior of her white cells.[12]

In another study involving imagery, researchers at Michigan State University found that students using guided imagery could improve the functioning of certain white cells called neutrophils. They could also decrease, but not increase, white cell counts. At one point in the study, a form of imagery intended to increase neutrophil count unexpectedly caused a drop instead. Subsequently, students were taught imagery explicitly intended to keep the neutrophil count steady, while increasing their effectiveness. Both goals were achieved.[13]

These studies suggest intriguing questions about whether it might be possible for people with CFS to deal with the problem of chronic immune activation through such methods. Could it be that by imagining the white cells becoming more relaxed and practicing the relaxation response themselves, their hyperactivity could be reduced?

The specificity hypothesis is not the only avenue being explored for how imagery may benefit immunity. Another point of view is the "general effect" hypothesis. This means that benefits can arise from the general overall *feeling of greater control* that comes when you believe you can influence your health through these methods, and as your confidence grows. There is evidence for this in studies where a sense of control over the source of stress has been linked to better immunity, compared to the sense of having no control.

For example, in a study at Stanford University, twenty subjects who were afraid of snakes agreed to have blood samples taken to test the changes in immune responsiveness as they got close to and, eventually, handled snakes. As their sense of mastery and confidence, or "self-efficacy" increased, their blood chemistry changed to reflect significantly better immune functioning.[14]

This increasing sense of self-efficacy may have been the factor at work in a study of cancer patients which found improvement in immunity associated with imagery practice.[15] Ten metastatic cancer patients attended monthly group sessions for a year in which they were supervised in imagery practice. Between sessions they performed the exercises twice a day. After each monthly meeting, blood samples were drawn to monitor immunologic changes. Significant improvements were found in several immune functions, including natural killer cell activity.[16]

If feelings of confidence or competence are really the key, then whatever method you choose—if you use it regularly—can contribute to restored balance in immune functioning. This is consistent with the advice of Carl Simonton, M. D., who once told me that if you feel hopeful, powerful, and optimistic after doing your imagery, then that is the criterion of success, much more than the details of the images used.[17] It follows that if you are confident in your ability to influence your health, *this confidence* will reduce the degree of stress you feel as a result of CFS. Then your healing can progress more readily.

Avoiding the Perils of Mind/Body Medicine

The explosive growth of interest in mind/body medicine has spawned a shift in our attitudes and beliefs about healing. However, in their enthusiasm to jump on the bandwagon, many popular books and magazines have fostered some erroneous beliefs which can lead to feelings of guilt, self-blame, confusion, despair, or hopelessness in people attempting to deal with CFS through a mind/body model. We can call this the "psychosocial morbidity" of mind/body medicine.

Some doctors take a conservative approach, discouraging patients from using complementary therapies for fear of the psychosocial morbidity which may result if the patient doesn't do well or if their condition deteriorates. This approach has its own risks, however, namely that the person may miss a helpful service; or worse, may interpret the physician's attitude as suggesting a hopeless situation, leading to false despair. Other physicians support complementary therapies but help the patient to explore their expectations to make sure they are realistic.

The way to avoid the risks is to have a realistic understanding of the benefits and limits of mind/body medicine. I have found five key principles of mind/body medicine to be sources of trouble for many people. While many of these principles are based on well-intentioned ideas, we need to refine our ways of thinking—our "paradigms"—to be more in step with the psychology of healing. I will discuss these from the point of view of shifting from old to new paradigms.

THE MEANING OF RESPONSIBILITY

You've probably heard these sayings: "Take responsibility for your health." "You are responsible for your health." "You are the creator of your health." The movement is away from the passive orientation ("Here, doctor, my health is none of my business, you take care of it"), and toward personal empowerment. Unfortunately some patients have followed this line of thinking to undesirable conclusions.

Old Paradigm:
Responsibility Means Ultimate Control and Ultimate Blame

Most of us grew up in a culture in which the word "responsibility" had a definite charge to it. As children we associated *ir*responsibility with misbehavior, punishment, blame, fault, shame, and guilt. It was often used in the context of discipline or threats of discipline at home or school. This old idea of "taking responsibility" is usually oriented to self-judgment for one's past behavior. By applying these attitudes to health, it's not difficult to see how some people conclude:

> Since I am responsible for my health, I must have given myself CFS. It's my fault, and it serves me right. I brought it on myself, and I must figure out why, so I can correct it. Whether I get well depends on how hard I work on myself . . .

New Paradigm: Responsibility as Here and Now

Rather than having a retrospective, punitive focus, responsibility is here and now, present tense. It has to do with how you live your life from this moment forward. In fact it's *ir*responsible to indulge in self-condemnation about the past. We probably would all have lived differently if we had known then what we know now, but that's not the case. Responsibility means responding here and now to the challenges you face, given the resources you have now, both inner and outer. This includes the intelligent use of medical treatment, as well as lifestyle change and self-help.

There can be value in looking at the past to see how we may have contributed to our vulnerability, especially if we engaged in risky or unhealthy behavior which continues today. This kind of looking within is done with an exploratory attitude toward life's lessons, not with a blameful attitude. If you remember the multicausal perspective, it's impossible to say to what extent past behavior contributed to the onset of CFS. To blame yourself about the past is a distraction from helping yourself *now*. The key is to shift from self-blame for the past to self-support for the present.

HOPE
Hope refers to a positive expectancy about the future with the belief that something better than the current circumstances is possible.[18] Its opposite is despair. In CFS this is especially important, since belief in recovery and in your ability to influence it are so central.

Old Paradigm: Statistical Odds Determine Hope
In the old paradigm, hope is considered a matter of statistical odds. Most illnesses have a predictable course and statistics have been generated about the length and stages of illness. People who hope for some different outcome other than what the statistics suggest would be subject to accusations of "false hope." This is especially true, of course, with illnesses such as advanced cancers or HIV where the prognosis is grim—even though people have been known to defeat the odds.

In a sense it is good that we do not yet have statistics about recovery time in CFS, for if we did, people might tend to assume that those statistics applied to them as individuals.

New Paradigm: Hope Amid Uncertainty
Hope can be separated from statistical odds. For example, a person may hope to defy the statistics, or that a cure will be discovered soon, while fully understanding the realistic nature of CFS. He can believe in the possibility of the unusual or unexpected.

Stories of people surviving normally fatal illnesses have inspired others to be hopeful where they may have not been before. And, of course, hope applies to dimensions other than just physical recovery. People can hope for healing emotionally, spiritually, and in relationships—even in a dying process.

In this paradigm, hope by its very nature cannot be false. However, it should exist alongside a realistic understanding of the challenge one faces. Hope can exist with *un*realistic understanding *as well as* with realistic understanding.

EMOTIONS
Emotions and emotional expression are often difficult areas for both patients and care-givers. As we have discussed, emotion plays an important role in host resistance and quality of life. However, the mind/body movement has seen a great deal of confusion and misleading advice about how to cope with strong and uncomfortable emotions.

Old Paradigm: Emotions as "Positive or Negative"
Our anti-emotional culture promotes the idea that emotions can be divided into positive and negative. Those that feel good and are pleasant (joy, love, happiness) are labeled positive, and those that feel bad or unpleasant (fear, sadness, anger) are labeled negative.

Many people who embrace this paradigm believe that emotions are an adversary to be mastered or controlled. It goes something like this:

> Negative emotions are bad for your health and positive emotions are good for your health, so get negative emotions out of your life in order to promote your healing. Negative emotions go against having a positive mental attitude which is necessary for healing. Don't feel negative emotions!

Unfortunately this conditioning goes very deep and is often shared by health-care providers. The result can be a subtle form of conspiracy between helper and patient in believing that there are "negative" emotions, and the patient then seeks to repress or suppress these authentic aspects of life.

New Paradigm: Emotion as Energy to Be Expressed
In the new paradigm, what's important is not attaching a positive or negative value to emotions. Rather it's emotional *expression* that influences health and quality of life. The need for expression ap-

plies to all emotions—anger, fear, and sadness *as well as* love and joy. Expression is health promoting, and suppression is health negating.

Rather than thinking of emotions as positive or negative, they are simply one expression of your life energy as it flows through you. Imagine a beam of light shining through a prism that separates the light into a rainbow of colors. The prism is the person, the beam of light his life energy, and the rainbow represents the array of colors that energy can take, or the emotions. Placing your finger on the prism to block out certain colors will disturb the flow of light through the prism, and yield a distorted rainbow. Likewise, attempting to disown or deny any aspects of your emotional experience will disturb the flow of life energy through you, and adversely affect your body's healing processes.

Many people benefit from freer expression, even to the point of catharsis (emotional release such as crying, or pounding cushions with a tennis racket, if appropriate). They often find tremendous relief and new stores of energy through emotional release.

POSITIVE MENTAL ATTITUDE
Often people think of their mental attitude as a weapon for influencing the course of illness.

Old Paradigm: Feel Good and Optimistic at All Times
Patients often have the belief that a positive mental attitude is health-promoting, and therefore they should strive at all times to display this. "Positive" is interpreted as meaning feeling only "positive emotions" and never allowing oneself to appear helpless, hopeless, or in despair (even if these feelings are actually present). Patients' efforts are often driven by a feeling of urgency and tension: "If I let down on my attitude, it will have dire consequences for my health." Often such beliefs are based on reading about links between depression and illness, or the healing power of laughter.

The old paradigm of the positive attitude usually goes hand in glove with the old paradigm of emotions. Of course there is value in maintaining an optimistic outlook. The difficulty arises when belief in the "positive mental attitude" becomes the rationale for suppressing emotions, denying needs, refusing to acknowledge symptoms, or withholding requests for support. Many people misconstrue this belief to mean we should disregard these aspects which we associate with our "dark side." Yet the willingness to embrace and express these aspects of ourselves can play a vital part in healing.

New Paradigm:
Positively Accept and Express All of Your Feelings

A truly positive attitude means having a positive attitude toward *all* your emotions. This means a positive acknowledgment, a positive acceptance, and a positive expression. You can positively embrace all that you are, and not judge or disown any authentic aspects of your experience, including acknowledgment of those times when you feel hopelessness or despair. Through this positive acceptance of all aspects of yourself, your energy is not bound up in the suppression or repression of feelings and is free to help with healing.

Perhaps you can recall a time in the past when you had what you'd call a good cry. Maybe you remember the feeling of freshness or lightness that occurred afterward. It may sound ironic, but the quickest way to free yourself from feelings of despair or hopelessness is by their full expression. Feelings are transitory if we allow them to be.

THE ROLE OF SELF-HELP

Patients often have the goal of mastering certain self-help techniques such as imagery or the relaxation response. They have read books or reports in which others attributed their recovery to these techniques, and have heard of research about the effects of such techniques on immunity. They usually do not understand that when such studies report "significant" effects of a technique, this simply means that a measurable impact has occurred, even though that impact may or may not be of a magnitude to influence physical well-being. Such studies are important for instilling hope about the possible pathways to influence health, but they do not guarantee healing for a given patient.

Old Paradigm:
Self-Help Is Curative, and Depends on My Performance

Difficulty arises from the belief that these techniques are themselves like a medical treatment. Hence the belief may be something like this:

> I'm going to learn to visualize, practice it regularly, and if I do it well enough, it will be successful in ridding me of CFS. If I don't get better, it will be because I didn't do the techniques well enough or often enough.

The problem is the belief that the technique itself is curative, and that one's performance is the determining factor of medical outcome. The person may then feel performance anxiety and fear of failure. If these feelings are present during daily practice, the person reinforces precisely those states of anxiety which the techniques are intended to help. Another way of saying this is that the "scared inner child" is the one who does the technique rather than the composed, adequate adult who sees the big picture and relaxes into the process.

New Paradigm: Self-Help as a Contribution

You can visualize perfectly and do everything right ten times a day, but there is no guarantee of what will happen medically. Such techniques must be seen as contributions to the overall program, but not as determining factors. They can in themselves be rewarding in terms of mood states, feelings of hope and optimism, reducing symptoms, and improving quality of life.

They are a way of taking responsibility to do the best you can with the resources you have now. They may also contribute to the overall flow of the healing process in the body, but they are not a panacea. The realistic perspective is to realize that self-help is an important contribution to the larger multicausal approach.

Living with Ambiguity

Throughout this book I have been stressing the multicausal perspective, and the idea that both the illness and your recovery are influenced by many combined factors. One difficulty with the multicausal perspective is its ambiguity. It certainly would be easier to organize your response to a single cause such as a virus, than to tolerate the ambiguity of being told the illness is multicausal and there is nowhere to lay the blame. In this ambiguity, some will tend to even blame themselves, for this at least gives them a focus for their anger.

Likewise, it is easier to place all your hope for recovery in a single medication or even a single self-help strategy. Yet, you must constantly remind yourself of the big picture in coping with this illness. Often it is necessary to close your eyes, take a deep breath, and remind yourself that you can only do the best you can do, bring all the pieces together that you can, and then be patient.

In the following chapters we will explore in greater depth self-help strategies that will help you take advantage of the mind/body connection.

8

The Healing Power
of Deep Relaxation

"I realized that my greatest enemy was not the infection, it was stress."   —Ginger

As evidenced by the research described in the previous chapter, the relaxation response is a profoundly healing state which arises from stilling your mind and body. It may be the most fundamental healing state of which you are capable.

The benefits of this special state are really the result of helping your body and mind rest deeply. When you are free of stress and tension, your body's inherent tendencies toward balance and harmony are given the opportunity to assert themselves. Every cell has within its nucleus a genetic code or blueprint, showing what perfect harmony, balance, and health look like for you. That blueprint contains detailed instructions for each individual cell as to its own role in restoring that state of balance.

I wish to emphasize here the importance of this genetic code. Imagine for a moment that you had the responsibility to direct all your body's functions. You must make a conscious effort to pump your blood, to digest your breakfast, to filter your blood through your liver and kidneys, to regulate your temperature, to grow white cells in your marrow, to direct each breath, etc. You would very quickly be overwhelmed with this responsibility. Fortunately your body has the programming to do all this for you.

You need not even be awake, and these vital functions will go on.

Likewise, all your body's healing responses go on without your conscious participation. When you have a cut or bruise, the cells in that area know exactly what to do to restore that area to health, to knit the tissue back together, to remove the debris, to clear away the bacteria, and to restore the area to its original condition—in accordance with the genetic code for that area. What an overwhelming responsibility it would be if you had to understand consciously how to do this!

The best you can do is support these inherent healing processes. And one of the most supportive things you can do is to remove as much interference as possible. To the degree that stress interferes with these healing processes, you will benefit by clearing the way for the relaxation response to work its magic.

The Wisdom of Fatigue

In CFS the relaxation response has particular importance. The experience of fatigue is caused by certain cytokines released by the immune system. These cytokines are detected by neural receptors throughout your body. These receptors send the message to the brain that there is an elevated presence of cytokines in the blood, and the brain responds by trying to slow you down. Why would the brain do this? Is the fatigue merely a mistake, an aberration which serves no purpose?

Let us consider the possibility that the fatigue is a purposeful response on the part of your body. It serves the purpose of getting you to rest. This is your body's way of getting the relaxation needed to allow healing to take place.

Remember, your body knows how to heal. You can respect the fatigue as an intelligent response. Rather than thinking of it as an inconvenience or an adversary, it is part of your body's effort to promote healing. Its intention is to allow the deep relaxation needed so your body can realign itself with its inborn programming. When you argue with your body—that is, when you attempt to go on and ignore the symptom—it will escalate and win. You cannot defeat the wisdom of your body.

What the Relaxation Response Is *Not*

There are a variety of popular images of what is meant by relaxation. To some people, it means lying on a sofa in front of the television. For others it means an evening at the movies, or reading a good book. For someone else it may mean taking a nap, or talking with friends. Perhaps the common denominator for most people is that it means not working or doing anything that is physically challenging.

However, none of these activities is likely to lead to the relaxation response. In fact, it may be safe to say that many people have never experienced true relaxation. This is because it involves more than just a state of rest for your body.

The relaxation response is a state of profound rest for both body and mind. This means that neither is active, which is why many people have not experienced it. The body may be in a state of repose, but the mind is another story. As long as your mind is busily engaged, your body is unable to totally relax. Every thought and feeling that passes through your mind has an effect on your body and its chemistry, however subtle.

This certainly applies to reading, television, and movies. Your mind is directly engaged, and is flooded with images which evoke reactions within you. This, of course, is the intention of such entertainment.

As people with CFS know all too well, you can sleep without necessarily having the benefits of deep relaxation. The sleep center in the brain is not functioning properly, and the anxiety and other symptoms of the illness can further impair your ability to have refreshing and restful sleep. Yet, sleep is the best your body can do on its own to approach the benefits of the relaxation response. The level of relaxation we seek is deeper than that attained in sleep, when your mind remains active, in the form of dreaming. If you can learn the art of creating this deeper state, then sleep will be much more beneficial.

The Key: Calming Your Mind

The key to creating the relaxation response is to calm your mind. A calm mind is a mind with minimal activity—little or no thinking, analyzing, fantasizing, or worry. The more calm your mind is, the deeper the state of relaxation is for your body. This may come as a surprise to some, but the fact is that you can be fully awake, aware, and alert while your mind is calm.

This, of course, forces you to examine your relationship to your mind. The most fundamental point you need to accept is that you are not your mind. In Western cultures you are led to assume that your mind is at the center of your being, it is the most essential part of you. Eastern cultures, however, have an alternative point of view—that your mind is on the periphery rather than at the center of you. In the center is your soul or spirit or consciousness, something more basic than your mind. And your mind itself is like an organ which you can activate or deactivate.

While this is a somewhat awkward way of saying it, my point is that it is possible to separate from, or dis-identify with, your mind. You can see yourself as having a relationship with your mind rather than simply *being* it. You must become interested in this relationship if you are to have any hope of being free of stressful thoughts and feelings, and their consequent ill effects in your body.

Calming the mind has been the province of mystics and spiritual seekers for thousands of years. This is because they have discovered that a busy mind is an obstacle to spiritual growth and insight. As a result, hundreds of traditions have evolved for calming it.

Most of the traditions involve some form of meditation, which many mind/body programs teach as a means to reduce stress and create the relaxation response. While such techniques originally developed for spiritual pursuits, it is a welcome side benefit that the states they induce can create the optimal conditions for healing to occur in your body.

In CFS, since your mind and its functioning can be affected by the syndrome, the realization that you can separate yourself from your mind will help you to retain a sense of power and volition; that you are not simply a helpless victim of the syndrome and its effects. When you can have some degree of mastery over this process, you can more easily accept that the syndrome is transitory, that symptoms come and go, and that healing is possible.

How to Lay the Groundwork

What I will present here are the common denominators of many different traditions for calming your mind.

WILLINGNESS TO PRACTICE REGULARLY

This endeavor involves the development of a skill. Regular practice is necessary to deepen your mastery of this skill. And with practice, your relaxation will deepen, will be achieved more rapidly, and the benefits will, of course, be greater. Regular practice means daily, ideally at a specified time, and for a specified period such as thirty or more minutes.

WILLINGNESS TO WORK WITH YOUR RESISTANCE

The nature of the mind is to remain active. It has a tremendous momentum to keep on thinking all kinds of thoughts. When you initially sit down to learn a practice for calming the mind, you will discover how strong this momentum is. You must constantly remember your intention to stay with the practice, for your mind will resist and prefer to remain active.

WILLINGNESS TO BE NON-JUDGMENTAL OF YOURSELF

One of the traps you need to avoid is evaluation or judgment of your performance. These judgments, coming of course from your mind, are in fact a way your mind can sabotage your efforts to calm it. Most likely you will have thoughts such as "I'm getting nowhere with this . . . This is boring . . . I can't do this . . . I'm not doing it right . . ." etc. It is absolutely predictable and natural to have these thoughts, but again they should be understood as part of the natural resistance of your mind, and you must not be distracted by these judgments. If you are not careful to remember this, you can be easily demoralized or dissuaded from further practice.

CREATING THE RIGHT ENVIRONMENT

This means attending to the physical surroundings. Ideally you can find a place in your home which can become your special place for practice. Perhaps a corner in your bedroom, or some other place that is reserved for this process. Have the space arranged to be comfortable—a special chair, or cushions arranged in a certain way, so that you can feel at peace in this place. This helps send a message to your mind that when you are in this place, this is what you do.

PREVENTING DISTRACTIONS

I consider three types of distractions especially important here: noise, other people, and telephones. Perhaps you can think of others. Remember, your mind prefers to remain active, and any of these distractions will be seized upon immediately by your mind if given the opportunity. The best advice is:

Noise

Avoid the interference of appliances, televisions, or other sources of noise. If you live with others, you *must* enlist their cooperation in maintaining quiet during your practice.

Other People

If necessary, place a "Do Not Disturb" sign on your door. Again, you must enroll the cooperation of others. Make sure you communicate to them the importance of respecting your quiet time. If you have small children, you may need to arrange help with this, for otherwise your ears will be tuned to the slightest hint of their needing attention from you.

Telephones

The first choice is unplugging the phone at the wall. This way there is no ringing, no clicking of machines, and no imagining in your mind about who is calling and what they may be saying. Using an answering machine is the second choice, and if you do use one, turn off the volume and ringer, if possible.

I cannot overemphasize the importance of the prevention of outer distractions. They are the easiest to overlook, and the most likely to sabotage your practice. You are doing yourself a wonderful favor by creating the opportunity for true relaxation to happen, and the fundamentals must be in place.

Techniques to Calm the Mind

Now that we have discussed the prerequisites, let us turn to specific techniques. The methods to harness the mind, slow it down, and bring it under control involve what is called "mindfulness." This means you focus your mind's attention in such a way that your mind is literally *full* of what is happening right *now*. In these experiences, you will get to know your mind more deeply than ever before, for you will be in a new relationship with it. Below are described some techniques that you may use to practice mindfulness, which in turn will help induce deep relaxation.

USING THE BREATH

You may choose to use the breath as the focus for your relaxation process. Each breath is long, slow, and deep, into the belly. Being mindful of the breath, you become a student of it, and concentrate all your attention on a particular aspect of the breath. There are several ways the breath can be used.

Watching the Breath

One method of watching is to focus on the expansion and relaxation of your belly. Notice how as you breathe in, the belly expands outward as the diaphragm moves down, making more room for the lungs. As you exhale, notice how the belly is drawn back in, as if the belly button is reaching to touch the front of your spine. Follow the rhythm of this in-and-out movement, like a circle with no beginning point, just a continuous circular motion. This movement of the belly is like that of a person rowing a boat across a lake, with the arms moving in a circular motion, each stroke flowing into the next, with no clear ending or beginning for each stroke.

Another method of watching is to focus on a point just inside your nostrils. Imagine that there are millions of tiny, sensitive nerve endings that can feel the air moving in across this area of tissue. You might think of the air as an ocean of billions of molecules, like marbles, all rolling over each other and over these nerve endings as they cascade down your windpipe into your lungs. Then the flow reverses, and this sea of marbles pours back out, again over those same nerve endings, as it leaves your body. And just as a tidal pool next to the ocean is constantly filled and emptied by the ebb and flow of the waves, so too the ocean of air constantly pours in and back out, through your nostrils. Maintain your focus on this area just inside the entrance.

Counting Breaths

This means counting each in-breath and each out-breath, in pairs. For example: (in-breath) one, (out-breath) one, (in-breath) two, (out-breath) two, repeating this process up to ten. When you reach ten you begin again at one. Whenever you realize you have been distracted by thought and have lost count (which will happen!), rather than trying to remember where you were, you begin again at one.

Beginning-Middle-End

Another approach with the breath is to focus on the beginning, middle, and end of each breath. This means that you conceive of the breath as having three segments, and you notice each of these segments, with each in-breath and with each out-breath. In other words, you notice the beginning, middle, and end of the in-breath, followed by the beginning, middle, and end of the out-breath. This too becomes a circular process, and you can fall into a comfortable rhythm of flowing in a circular motion.

It is important in all the breathing techniques to use your senses, rather than just doing it as an intellectual exercise. Really focus your senses on the experience of each breath as intimately as you can. Feel the texture of the air, feel the rising and falling of your belly, the expansion of your rib cage as the ribs open like fingers on a hand with each breath. . . . It is this use of the senses that will help you stay focused on the process and, in turn, calm the mind. Fritz Perls, M.D., the father of gestalt therapy, once used a phrase which captures this process: "Lose your mind, and come to your senses."[1]

USING WORDS OR SOUNDS

Another method is to use a sound or word as the subject of your focus. This involves the repetition of the sound or word throughout the relaxation process. This too can be done in a variety of ways. One is to repeat the word on the out-breath. You can use a simple word, something which does not engage the mind, such as "one" or "ohm" or any other word which has a calming effect on you.

An alternative in this approach is to use a phrase which has a reassuring effect, such as "I am one," "I am calm," or "healing now." There are many variations of this technique possible, but they all have in common the repetition of the sound or words. You can choose any word or phrase that appeals to you. Just be careful that it is not something that engages your mind or stimulates thinking. The emphasis is on simplicity. The experience of repetition has a calming effect on your mind because it fills your mind and holds your focus throughout the process.

USING "PROGRESSIVE RELAXATION"

A favorite technique of many people is called "progressive relaxation." This involves a block of time and a quiet place, just like the earlier techniques described. However, your body itself is used as the focus of your attention. The aim is the same—that is, to disconnect from thought and spend a period of time in a state of deep relaxation of both body and mind.

Progressive relaxation may be done either lying down or sitting. In either case, you find a comfortable position, one from which you will not need to move for twenty or thirty minutes. Observe the same fundamentals described earlier in preparing the environment and having a special place.

This technique involves focusing on various parts of your body, relaxing them one by one, spending approximately a minute in each area. You tense, hold, and then release the muscles of a particular area, before moving on to the next area. Hold or clench the muscles in the area for a count of ten, and then release for a count of ten, before moving on to the adjacent area.

In a variation of this technique, you can forgo the tensing and releasing of muscles, and instead focus on simply bringing your awareness to each area and imagining that area softening and melting, releasing any tension that was present. Below is a relaxation exercise using this variation.

EXERCISE

Allow about twenty minutes to move through this process. Find a comfortable position, in an environment where you will not be disturbed or distracted.

Begin by closing your eyes and bringing your awareness to your breath. Take a few moments to breathe deeply and fully, emphasizing the length of the out-breath, letting it be long, deep, and thorough. After a few minutes when you feel your breathing has softened, bring your awareness to the toes of your right foot. Imagine that you can direct your breath into your toes, and as you breathe, your toes are softening and melting, letting go of any remaining tension. After a few breaths, bring your awareness to the rest of your right foot, and breathe into the entire foot, allowing it to soften, melt, and let go of any remaining tension.

Now let this feeling of softening and melting spread up through your right ankle, and bring your awareness to your right calf muscle. Again breathing slowly into this area, feeling it soften and melt with each full deep breath. Spend a few moments sensing the feeling of softness and melting, and then let this feeling of relaxation slowly move up through your right knee into your right thigh, and again, feel your right thigh muscles softening and melting, just letting go of any remaining tension . . .

Continue this process through the major muscle groups of your body, taking your time in each area (about a minute) until you feel a definite softening and melting sensation. Move from the right thigh to the hip, the buttocks, over to the left hip, down into the left thigh, knee, calf, ankle, foot, and toes. Then move up through the pelvis, lower back, middle, and upper back. Then around to the lower abdomen, solar plexus, rib cage, and chest. Then out to the shoulders, down the arms, the hands, to the finger tips. Move to the neck, throat, up the sides and back of the head, over the top of the scalp. Then down into the forehead, into the sinuses, eyes and eye sockets, cheeks, and mouth. Inside the mouth to the jaw muscles, the tongue, and the lips.

Now scan the entire length of your body, to see if there are any remaining areas with the slightest tension. Direct your breath into those areas, and with a long, thorough out-breath, let it all go . . .

Now rest. You are encouraged to experiment with both methods of the progressive relaxation technique and find which works best for you.

Handling Your Mind's Resistance

The greatest challenge to relaxation is staying focused, whether it be on the breath, word, sound, or parts of your body. And, of course, the source of this challenge is your mind, for it has a tremendous momentum toward continuous thinking. Your mind will go through a variety of strategies to distract you and engage you in its meandering ways. This may include continuously offering you its analysis about the process, as in "I'm not getting this . . . I'm doing great . . . How much longer? What time is it?"

If that doesn't capture your attention away from the process, your mind may try thinking about the important issues or problems in your life, or resort to showing reruns of horror movies about your illness. Its basic attitude will be, "Why waste this valuable time that could be put to constructive use, thinking about how to solve these problems?" Or it may choose to focus upon the details of daily living: "Let's see, how full is the gas tank? When did I balance the checkbook last? What do I need to pick up at the store?" Your mind will find both subtle and not-so-subtle ways to distract you and engage you in thought.

RETURNING HOME (AGAIN AND AGAIN)

Each time you discover you have lost your focus and have been caught up by your mind, your reaction is critical to the relaxation process. It is not realistic to expect that you should remain free of thought through the process and never succumb to your mind's seduction. The process is not one of attaining a fixed state of no-mind. Rather, it is a process of continuously and methodically returning back home to the meditation subject.

Some people find it helpful to imagine they are sitting by a riverbank, and the thoughts are merely debris floating by. They do not need to jump in and float down the river with the debris. Or you may imagine the thoughts are merely clouds drifting across the sky, as you notice them and return to your focus.

At first you may find that you stay focused for only a few seconds at a time before thoughts start crowding their way in. And each time you find yourself in thought, you simply return, as if to say "Oh, yes, back to the breath . . ." There is no need for judgment of yourself or analysis of the thought. Just keep returning back to the focus.

This is when to be especially wary of self-evaluation, for if you persist with a judgmental attitude toward yourself or your performance, you will experience meditation as one insult after another because you will quickly see that your expectations do not hold.

LABELING YOUR THOUGHTS
One strategy that may help you get some distance from your thoughts is to label them when they arise. Each time you find yourself captivated in thought, you take a step back and give that thought a descriptive label. You need only have a very short list of categories for, after all, most of your thoughts deal with a limited range of issues.

You may use any labels you find useful. You could use a simple scheme such as worry, fear, desire, thinking, fantasy or other labels. The point is to distance yourself a little from the thought, and attaching a label can help you shift your focus back to your practice. For example, when you suddenly realize you have wandered off to your bank balance, you might just attach the label "worry" to that line of thought. Then you immediately bring your awareness back to the focus of the technique you are using.

The Use of Music

Many people enjoy using music in relaxation, and it can certainly have a soothing effect on your mind and emotions. However, music can both help and hinder your creating the relaxation response. One must be careful in how one uses it, and what music is selected.

There are certain guidelines for this. Remember, since your intention is to calm your mind and body, it is best to select music which does not engage your mind in following a melody. While this may feel pleasant, it does not help in making your mind be still so the relaxation response can arise. On the other hand, music which is simple and non-intrusive, such as involving long tones or ocean waves gently lapping on the shore, and no melody that compels you to participate in it, can have a calming effect for your mind and facilitate the relaxation response. Some people find that music is helpful to relax deeply in the early stages of learning but then later becomes a distraction as they become more adept at calming the mind on their own.

With time and practice, you will find that your skill in attaining the relaxation response will increase noticeably. You will find the gaps between thoughts become wider, you will catch yourself more quickly, and less and less effort is required to return to your focus. You will also begin to notice patterns or characteristic types of thought that seem to keep arising, and this recognition will make it even easier to detach from them.

Ultimately you will discover deeper feelings of calm and peace than you thought possible. Finally, after each session you will find that your thinking is more clear and insightful. These are all worthwhile benefits which will add to the physiological benefits of the relaxation response.

9

Imagery and CFS

*"I visualize every day. I picture good things, seeing myself do things
I'd love to do, like swimming in Hawaii, soaking in my hot tub,
dancing . . . I visualize fulfilling goals, even tiny ones. Like planting
flower seeds tomorrow morning."* —Debbie

Can you picture yourself healthy? Can you actually imagine life
after CFS? Can you imagine what a life of balance, harmony, and
health will look like for you when you are well? In Chapter 7 we
reviewed some of the research showing that imagery can affect
immunity and healing. Now I would like to show you how you can
use this approach with CFS.

We all practice imagery, constantly. When you drive home, you
have a map in your mind which you follow. When you walk around
your house, you are following a map. What you "know," you know
in images. This is the language of the brain. When you see someone
you know, it is their image you recognize. Your images are also
constantly affecting your body. If you were abused as a child, you
may carry a subconscious image of yourself as a vulnerable child
about to be hit at any moment. You may hold your shoulders in a
tight, protective posture as your defense against this possibility.

The power of imagery can be harnessed as a self-help tool. It has
proven to be useful for many illnesses ranging from cancer to AIDS

to heart disease. In my practice, I have seen people with CFS benefit from imagery in several ways.

Learning from Drawing

Using drawings or images can help you clarify issues in your life. Often in my self-help programs we use drawings to reveal the person's inner attitudes and beliefs about what is happening. This can lead to useful insights about needed changes.

For example, during a group imagery session, Mary Ann drew a picture of herself being subdued by CFS, which was represented by a monster. Seeing this drawing, she realized how victimized she felt, and she immediately became in touch with her anger at this situation. Her anger fueled a renewed determination to break her old habit of volunteering to do all the legwork for her support group, which had been draining her of energy she needed to combat her illness.

This was the beginning of a much needed shift in her life—to stop doing favors for others that she really did not want to do. That shift has endured beyond her illness.

Imagery and Belief in Recovery

Imagery can help you strengthen your belief in recovery. Clinical experience has taught me that belief in recovery is a prerequisite in healing from CFS. Very often, however, I meet people who are seeking help, but cannot actually imagine themselves recovered. Whenever I begin working with someone, whether it is individually or in group programs, I address this issue.

We touched upon reasons why people have problems envisioning themselves healthy in Chapter 1. A major source of the difficulty is the powerful images of debilitation portrayed by the media. Unfortunately, the media's concentration on these negative images is not balanced by a presentation of images of healing, or the quiet triumphs of people who have recovered.

We are faced with a similar problem in media coverage of the AIDS crisis. Although people have recovered from AIDS and even converted from HIV positive back to HIV negative, this kind of news is not consistent with the popular imagery or beliefs about AIDS, so it simply goes unacknowledged. One rare exception to this is the story of my colleague and friend Niro Asistent, who made the cover of *New Age Magazine* in October 1991.

The ability to imagine yourself well affects you in many ways. On the physical level, the biochemistry of hope is very different from that of despair, and your immune responsiveness is affected by both. On the psychological level, a great deal of change in behavior is necessary to promote healing. Without belief in recovery, there is no incentive to sincerely follow through with such changes. And also, in those moments when you are in despair, feeling your absolute worst, imagery can be a resource to get you through.

One of the best ways to strengthen your belief in recovery is to create images of yourself well, and view them each day. Now that you understand the nature of CFS and the major principles in promoting recovery, you can create images which should be both realistic and inspiring to you.

Try the following exercises. Depending on your state at the moment, different exercises may serve you better than others. The object is to create images which you can call upon repeatedly. The first time you do these exercises, allow more time to develop the images. Once you have developed them, then you will be able to call upon them any time you want a shot of inspiration.

For each of the imagery techniques described, note that there are three stages. Stage one is to begin with a period of calming relaxation. Close your eyes and take several breaths to clear your mind of the clutter of the day so you can be fully present for the process at hand. Refer to Chapter 8 for help in calming your mind. It is essential to take this time to relax so that all your attention is available to the imagery.

The second stage is the healing imagery itself. Feel free to let your images change. As your healing work progresses, and as you get to know yourself better, your images will naturally evolve and change. Be open to this and whatever messages you can glean from these changes.

Finally, it is always good to end with imagery of yourself healed, doing something you love to do. This reinforces the sense of momentum and direction for your healing process. This is where you are headed, and this is the incentive for the earlier healing imagery. Be sure to include this each time.

EXERCISE 1. AFTER CFS: LIVING A LIFE OF BALANCE
The first time you do this exercise, take about twenty to thirty minutes to develop the imagery. Close your eyes, and take several long, slow, deep calming breaths.

Now create an inner movie of how you imagine your life will look after you have recovered from CFS. Include the following details:

How do you look?
How is your body different?
How are your eating habits different?
How do you moderate your energy now?
How is your pattern of exercise?
How is your pattern of working hours?
What kind of work are you doing?
With whom do you relate?
How is your communication with them?
How is the quality of your relationships different?
What kinds of people do you spend more time with? Less time?
How is your honesty and self-expression?
What are your goals?
How do you maintain your environment?
What do you appreciate about your life?

Now draw a picture of yourself that can represent your living this life of balance. This can be a picture you can hang on your refrigerator or a wall in your home.

EXERCISE 2. WHAT MAKES YOUR HEART SING?
Close your eyes, and take several long, slow, deep, calming breaths. Now imagine yourself totally healthy, doing something you love to do, something that makes your heart sing. Whether it is swimming

in the ocean, playing a musical instrument and singing, walking in nature, making love, dancing, fishing, or playing with children, find some activity that truly arouses joyful feelings within you.

In this inner movie, let yourself enjoy it to the hilt, more than you ever have before. Immerse yourself in the pleasant feelings and sensations. Let your images be vivid enough that these feelings well up within you. Remind yourself that you are worthy of happiness and fulfillment.

End by drawing a picture with as much detail as possible. This can be a picture you can hang on your refrigerator or a wall in your home.

EXERCISE 3. LOOKING BACK ON CFS

Close your eyes, and take several long, slow, deep, calming breaths. Now picture yourself in the future, five years after recovery from CFS. During those five years since you recovered, you have been able to contemplate what you learned and how you grew from that adversity.

Now imagine you are sitting on the ground in a meadow, with a circle of people. It is a beautiful day, and the nature that surrounds you seems most approving of your presence. The circle of people includes your closest friends, family members, teachers, and all the significant people of your lifetime. Be sure to include everyone with whom you have ever had an important relationship. The circle may even be two or three persons deep, so everyone can be included. Take a few minutes to fill out this circle.

Now give an informal talk entitled "My Healing Journey." It is about your past experience with CFS. Begin the talk with the following: "I'd like to tell you a story. I'd like to share with you what I learned and how I grew from having CFS . . ."

After finishing the talk, imagine that the circle of people offers you a gift. This gift symbolizes their appreciation for your being in their lives and sharing your story with them. Express your gratitude. Accept the gift graciously, and hold it close to your heart.

Now draw a picture of this gathering in the meadow. Attach names to the figures who represent all the important people of your life. Place this drawing on your refrigerator or a wall in your home.

Imagery and the Body

The following exercise will show you how and why imagery can physically affect your body.

EXERCISE 4. IN THE KITCHEN

Do this process slowly. Close your eyes, and take several long, slow, deep, calming breaths. Imagine for a moment that you are standing in the center of your kitchen. Slowly turn in a circle, and see the familiar items in the room. You may notice dishes in the sink, the toaster on the counter, the cupboards, the dishwasher . . . you may hear water dripping in the sink, the wall clock ticking. Notice the stove, the oven, the dials, and any pots or pans in view. Close your eyes now and get a clear image of your kitchen surroundings. To first complete this exercise, it's helpful to have someone read the following directions to you.

Now imagine you are turning toward the refrigerator. Look at the hardware on the door, the handle, and the color. Now slowly reach for the door and take the handle. Feel the texture of the handle. Is it cool, or warm? Smooth or rough? Now very slowly apply pressure to pull the handle toward you, and feel the door beginning to open. You may hear the breaking of the suction of the gasket around the door as it separates from the frame of the refrigerator. You may feel a rush of cool air around your ankles, and you may see the light come on inside.

Looking into the refrigerator now, notice the different kinds of food on the shelves. And notice if there are drawers containing other food. Take a moment to do a brief inventory of what you see. Now imagine you see a lemon sitting in the back, behind some other items. Reach over and back, grasp the lemon and bring it out.

Close the door and turn to step back toward the center of the kitchen. Now feeling this lemon in your hand, notice the nub on the end, and notice the rough texture of the skin. Squeeze the lemon lightly, and feel how it gives under your fingers.

Next, turn toward the counter and find a cutting board and a long sharp knife there. Placing the lemon on the cutting board, poise the knife over the center of the lemon. Now run the knife through the lemon, slicing the lemon in half. Feel how easily the knife glides through.

Setting the knife down now with half the lemon, take the other half and hold it up at eye level. As you look across the smooth cut surface, notice how there are tiny beads of juice resting on the sheen of the flat surface.

Next, squeeze the lemon slightly and watch as a tiny mist escapes up from the surface into the air. Now bring the surface toward your mouth, stick out your tongue, and run your tongue over the surface . . .

Notice now what is going on in your mouth. If you notice any increase in saliva, your imagination is working. But how does this occur? How did the images of the lemon cause your salivary glands to respond?

Obviously, there must be some pathway of influence between your brain and your salivary glands. That pathway is your nervous system. And what has happened is that the images you created in your mind triggered certain nerve impulses which were sent from your brain to your salivary glands and told them to prepare for lemon juice. The glands responded, not to the presence of real lemon juice, but to the image in your mind.

Just as you have nerve endings reaching into your salivary glands, you also have nerve endings reaching into your bone marrow, thymus, spleen, lymph nodes, muscles, and all other tissues of your body. It is through this system of "wiring" that imagery is able to affect the tissues and organs of the body. This is the same wiring that allows sexual arousal to take place with no physical stimulation.

Yet this is not the only means by which images can affect the body. Another is through chemical substances produced by the brain tissue. In addition to being the seat of the nervous system, the brain is also a gland. It manufactures many more kinds of drugs than could ever be found in any pharmacy. Your brain routinely transforms thoughts into chemical by-products, releasing them into the bloodstream.

If you are dwelling on images of debilitation and hopelessness, this is your imagery practice, and, as all images do, it has its own unique chemical by-products. If you practice the imagery of hope, you send a different chemistry into your body.

Specific Healing Imagery

"I can actually physically feel changes in my body when I do the visualization and imagery. That physical change takes away the anxiety I feel with this illness." —Ginger

The essence of using specific imagery to heal the body is to invent a way to *symbolize* what you want to have happen. The symbols need not necessarily be visual, like a photograph. They may use the other senses as well, such as feelings, sounds, tastes, or smells. The point is to create a symbolic experience in which the actions you want to take place are taking place now, and you can sense evidence of it happening.

For instance, in cancer and AIDS there is an adversarial process between white cells and cancer cells or viruses. The white cells are predators, and cancer cells or viruses are their prey. At the cellular level, what is needed is determination, aggressiveness, and discernment in the immune system to root out and remove the pathogens.

It is fairly easy to come up with symbols to represent this process. Imagine a pack of wolves chasing down rats in a field and gobbling them up. As you watch the wolves at work, you see how they cooperate with each other to circle around the rats and close in for the kill. The wolves use their very keen senses, their intelligence, and teamwork to clear the field of the rats. What is left behind is a clean, healthy field. One cancer patient would practice this imagery while driving on the freeway. In the privacy of her own car, she would growl, gnash her teeth, and even salivate as she devoured the little critters.

The healing process in CFS is not quite as simple as the adversarial approach. At this writing, we are not sure what the disease process looks like, though we know the symptoms are the effects of chronic immune activation. If on-going activity of a virus is what causes this process, then the aggressive kind of imagery used in cancer and AIDS would be appropriate.

However, it may also be a "hit-and-run" virus, one that did its damage and then left the immune system stuck in a state of overactivation, unable to recover long after the virus was gone or became inactive. If this is so, then the symbolic themes for healing may be different. Whereas in the first case, you would want your immune responses to be more active and powerful, in the second case, you would want them *less* active and *less* powerful.

Coming Back into Balance

There is a simple solution to this ambiguity. An immune system out of balance is not as effective against viruses as one which is in balance. You can deal with both issues—the possibility of an active virus, and the chronic immune overactivation—by restoring overall integrity and harmony in the immune system.

Rather than getting too absorbed in scientific details, it is best to settle on general themes. A focus on harmony, rhythm, and balance is suggested. Following are some imagery processes to deal with these themes.

EXERCISE 5. YOU, THE MAESTRO

Spend fifteen or twenty minutes with this process. Close your eyes, and take several long, slow, deep, calming breaths. Now imagine you are an orchestra conductor. Perhaps you are the eminent director of an internationally known philharmonic in your name. You have a vast, talented, well-equipped orchestra, with all the essential players. They are loyal to you and have devoted their entire careers, indeed their lives, to making beautiful music for you.

In this orchestra you have the full range of instruments, which can make a tremendous variation in sounds. When they are playing in harmony and rhythm with each other, the music is truly beautiful. Imagine, however, that the orchestra has fallen into disarray. The tuba section is playing full blast, while the flute section is being drowned out.

What will you say to your orchestra? How will you get them back into harmony?

Playing classical music is a good way to develop this imagery. You might experiment with a beautiful, perhaps methodical piece such as Ravel's *Bolero* for this. With the music playing softly in the background, close your eyes and practice directing your orchestra. Enjoy the feeling of harmony that arises in you when you immerse yourself in the music. And imagine that the orchestra represents your immune system, with all its players, having restored a state of harmony and balance. Listen very closely, more closely than ever before in your life, to discover what true harmony is. Feel the vibrations of the sound penetrating all the way into your marrow, the birthplace of your white cells. Become intimately familiar with the concept of harmony.

Now end by picturing yourself healthy, doing something you love to do.

EXERCISE 6. HEALING YOUR WHITE CELLS

In the chapter on the relaxation response I made the point that relaxation is a state in which all the body's healing mechanisms function at their maximum. The chemistry of stress disturbs healing, and the chemistry of relaxation supports it.

We observed that every cell in your body has a genetic code which defines its role in your health. This genetic code can be thought of as an image which is carried in the heart of every white cell. In CFS certain white cells have fallen out of alignment with their own internal image, and are malfunctioning. Some are hyperaroused, and some are depressed or inhibited.

In this process, you use the relaxation response to benefit the white cells themselves. Close your eyes, and take several long, slow, deep, calming breaths. For a few minutes, use your favorite method of creating the relaxation response in your body as a whole.

Now picture your white cells (or a symbol for them) going through a relaxation experience. Imagine your white cells taking long, slow, calming, deep breaths. Imagine them exhaling any tension or negativity they might have accumulated. Imagine them releasing the forces of disease with each out-breath. Assist them in this with your own breathing.

Feel how this relaxation has a calming effect on the white cells. Feel how their tension melts away. Feel how their exaggerated state of arousal slowly drifts back down toward balance, as they rest more deeply. For those which are depleted and exhausted, feel how the deep breathing and profound rest help them restore themselves. Feel their energy building, like a marathon runner resting on a tropical island after several long weeks of intense training.

Stay focused on the deep, calm breathing. Imagine every cell is breathing with you, and that as deeply as you go into a state of healing relaxation, your white cells go just as deep. Spend a while in this healing state, letting your white cells soak up the benefits of deep relaxation.

Now end by picturing yourself healthy, doing something you love to do.

EXERCISE 7. THE GOLDEN HEALING LIGHT

Allow about fifteen to twenty minutes for this exercise. Close your eyes, and take several long, slow, deep, calming breaths. Now imagine that hovering just a few inches above your head is a golden ball of healing light. You may even feel a sensation of warmth or tingling on your scalp below this ball of healing light. As you continue with your long, slow, deep breathing, allow this golden ball of healing light to slowly descend toward the top of your head.

Feeling the sensations grow slightly stronger, let the golden ball of healing light now begin to penetrate the top of your head. Feel it entering the top of your skull and filling your head with its golden healing warmth. Let its golden healing light reach into all the tissues and cells inside your head, filling them all with golden healing warmth.

Feel the golden ball of healing light now slowly descending further down into your neck and throat areas, filling them with warmth and golden light. Now, like a thick, lazy liquid, let it spread further down into your chest and out toward your shoulders. Feel the golden healing warmth now spreading down through your upper arms, slowly pouring its way down into your forearms, through your wrists, into your hands. Everywhere this golden healing light goes, it penetrates into the deepest levels, all the way into your marrow. Let it fill your marrow with golden healing light.

Imagine the golden ball of healing light now moving down through your rib cage, expanding outward in all directions, and slowly descending down into your abdomen, filling all your internal organs with golden healing light. With each breath, you can reinforce the healing power of this golden light penetrating every cell.

Moving down now into your lower abdomen, through your pelvis, out to your hips . . . fill all these areas with this magnificent golden healing warmth, and now letting this golden healing warmth begin to pour down into your thighs, through the marrow of your long thigh bones, down through your knees, into your calves . . . finding its way through your ankles, into your feet, and filling your feet, all the way to the tips of your toes.

Now let this golden healing light become centered in the middle of your chest, so that with each breath you take, you reinforce its glow, just as an ember glows brighter when you breathe into it.

Realize that no virus can withstand the intensity of this golden healing light. Viruses simply dissolve and vaporize under this light. You might even hear a hissing or fizzing sound as your entire body is cleared of viruses through the powerful action of this light. Even those viruses which were hiding out inside cells are vaporized. There is no escape.

Know that you can send this golden healing light throughout your body, your marrow, your immune system, and each white cell, simply by closing your eyes and breathing into it. . . . Know that every white cell drinks in this golden healing light with every full breath you take.

Now end by picturing yourself healthy, doing something you love to do.

EXERCISE 8. FIGHTING SPIRIT

Use this exercise if you feel drawn to the imagery of an adversarial confrontation between you and the forces of illness. If you believe that you are fighting a virus, or if you feel anger, disgust, or rage toward the illness, this kind of imagery can help you channel your fighting spirit. Of course, I am only outlining the process below. After you learn the steps of the exercise, you will be able to adapt it to your own imagery in the future.

Now take a few minutes to choose two symbols: one to represent the forces of illness and one to represent the forces of healing. It is recommended that you use living creatures, since they can more easily arouse powerful, primal feelings in the subconscious. If you use more abstract images like lights, stars, machines, or inanimate objects, these usually do not carry as much emotional charge. A strong emotional charge is empowering.

If you use people, even a kind of people you consider bad, there may still be some ambivalence about doing what you need to do to get rid of them. Use symbols in which the contrast between the forces of darkness and light is very strong and easy to grasp.

For example, to represent the forces of illness, you might use creatures such as maggots, worms, insects, or rats. They are trying to invade and dominate your life. They have absolutely no regard for your well-being. They have no respect for you, nor any interest in negotiation, discussion, or compromise. Their behavior toward you is disgusting and destructive. If they had their way, they would destroy your health, and ultimately even take your life from you.

To represent the forces of healing, choose a symbol that has the qualities of intelligence, sharp senses, swift movement, cleverness, aggressiveness, and lethal, undeniable power. You want your defenders to be overwhelming, decisive, and thorough in their protection of you. Examples might include a pack of wolves, sharks, polar bears, eagles, piranha, or other powerful creatures. All your defenders are totally and completely loyal and devoted to your well-being. You are their master. Remember, the white cells function by killing invaders, according to nature's laws of predators, prey, and the survival of the fittest.

Once you have selected your symbols, close your eyes, and take several long, slow, deep calming breaths. Now picture a scene in which the disease process is taking place. See the symbols of darkness, doing whatever you imagine they do in your body. Take your time to work out a scenario that represents this. You might even draw a picture that shows what the disease activity looks like.

After you have developed your imagery of the illness, begin to introduce your healing forces. Bring them into the picture and see how they confront and destroy the forces of illness. See that your healing forces are intelligent, overwhelmingly powerful, and thorough in wiping out their prey. See how they are well-organized and cooperate with each other, as they root out and destroy the vermin. Now take your time to be sure all the invaders have been vanquished. Once you are certain of this, see your protectors strutting around, triumphantly celebrating.

Now take a few moments to give a speech of gratitude to your protectors. Let them know how much you appreciate their efforts. After all, they are willing to give their lives for you, if that is what it takes to protect you from the forces of illness. Thank them and praise them profusely.

Now shift to another scene. This time, picture yourself healthy, happy, fully recovered, doing something you love to do—whatever makes your heart sing. This, after all, is the goal, the incentive for which all your protectors have been working. Take your time to truly feel the feelings of pleasure and fulfillment that come from being healthy and doing what you truly love to do.

Common Questions About Imagery

How do I know whether it's working?
How you feel afterward will tell you to what degree your imagery is serving you. In fact, this is more important than the details of the images you use. If you feel triumphant, uplifted, empowered, more energetic, more relaxed, more confident, these are all beneficial states. Remember, the purpose of imagery is to have impact on your chemistry. All these shifts in your subjective feelings reflect shifts in your chemistry, and they are the evidence that you are on the right track.

Is there a right way to do imagery?
As stated above, the most important criterion is how you feel afterward. You can be following all steps properly, but if you don't have a *subjective experience* of feeling better or uplifted afterward, then you need to change something. The only right way is the way that brings you these subjective results.

How often should I do imagery?
The more often you practice, the more familiar the images will become to you and the more deeply they will be embedded in your subconscious. When the subconscious fully embraces these images and the attitudes they represent, it will work around the clock to bring your life more into alignment with what these images represent.

For this reason, it is good to have a routine for yourself of at least once a day, at a given time and place, for your practice. If you can do it three times per day, that is even better. Also, rather than the formal three-step process, you can "check in" with your images several times during your day, for just a few moments. Sitting on the toilet, driving in your car (with eyes open!), anytime you feel the impulse to, check in and reinforce your imagery.

What about tapes?

If you find a tape whose voice and images you feel drawn to, then go ahead and use it. However, your own images may be preferable to someone else's, because they originate in your own sub-conscious and will have the greatest meaning for you. (See Appendix C for information on tapes for CFS by the author.)

One suggestion is to make your own tape. Write out a script that includes everything you want in your imagery. Then record it, taking care to leave plenty of pauses to develop the images as you go along. Also be sure to include all three stages in the tape, with the introductory relaxation and the triumphant ending.

I can't draw. Is drawing really necessary?

No, it is not necessary. However, it can be helpful. Realize that your drawings are not going to be entered into any art contest and do not judge them, for this might dissuade you from using them. Also, understand that the drawings are just a rough approximation of your images. They simply serve the purpose of suggesting or reminding you of certain themes and attitudes. Have fun with them, and don't take them too seriously.

My attention wanders. What to do?

It is natural for your attention to wander during meditation, relaxation, and imagery. This is not a problem. When you discover this has happened, simply bring your awareness back to the imagery and resume where you left off. There is no need to judge yourself about this, for there is nothing wrong with it. It is only a problem if you are nonaccepting of this.

My images change a lot. Should I be consistent?

It is comforting to have consistency, and you will probably settle on favorite images that will stay with you for some time. However, your images will naturally change as you change, as your health situation changes, and as you gain more insight about your own healing process.

I don't see pictures in my mind. Can I still use imagery?
Imagery is a broad concept that embraces all the senses. Some people's images are more pictorial, while others image more in terms of feelings, sounds, or other sensations. All of these are equally valid. The sound of a pack of wolves howling at the moon, or the feeling of the golden healing light melting away and vaporizing any remaining viruses can also be effective images.

10
Breath, Energy, and Emotion

"I feel great. I have more energy now than I've had in weeks. And normally I'm wiped out at this time of day."
—John, through his tears, after a group breathing exercise late one afternoon at 7000 feet.

In my clinical experience with CFS I have found breathing, energy, and emotion to be intimately related. While I have touched on them several times already, I feel they warrant a separate chapter because of their importance. In this chapter I will discuss how they complement each other. I will then present some exercises you can use on your own to create more energy through the breath.

Energy

Healing takes energy. Ironically, conventional Western medicine does not actually have much to say about what energy is or how it works. However, Oriental medicine has made a science of the body's energy for thousands of years. Here are some general principles of Oriental medicine which I believe are especially relevant to CFS:

1. The body we live in is an energy system. Life-force energy, or "chi," is constantly flowing and circulating through our organs and along energy pathways called "meridians."

2. We are vulnerable to disease because of blockages, imbalances, or deficiencies in the flow of energy through the body. The flow of energy can be disturbed by many things, including too little or too much of certain food substances, too little or too much exercise, chronic emotional or physical stress, environmental toxins, drugs or alcohol, or other unhealthful habits.

3. When the body's defenses must face a pathogen such as a virus, cancer cell, or bacteria, it takes "chi" to fuel the response. If not enough "chi" is available, disease can ensue. In Oriental medicine, CFS is considered a "chi" deficiency disease. Assuming CFS is triggered by a virus, then the immune system was not able to subdue the virus and prevent it from doing its damage. It now takes "chi" for the immune system to heal itself, return to normal, and, if the virus remains in the system, keep it in a latent state.

4. We are all endowed with an abundance of "chi" at birth. We can strengthen our chi in several ways, including nutrients, herbal medicine, treatments such as acupuncture, and a variety of self-help exercises, some of which will be presented later. Two of the most immediate ways you can work with your energy on a moment-to-moment basis are with fuller breathing and emotional expression, both of which we'll discuss.

Emotion

In Chapter 7 I used the analogy of a beam of light passing through a prism and coming out as a rainbow of colors. The light represented basic life-energy, the prism represented the person, and the colors represented the range of emotions. I would like to reiterate that all emotions are expressions or variations of the same basic energy source. When we attempt to interfere with the flow of life-energy through us—that is, when we try to deny or deaden ourselves to particular emotions—we distort the entire flow of our life-energy.

We have all grown up in a culture in which emotion is poorly understood. Most of us have been taught that this mysterious, powerful, and sometimes unpredictable energy is something to be controlled, since control represents a form of "mastery." Much of our early childhood conditioning around this energy was to limit its expression. Unfortunately, this attitude has pitted us against our emotions, resulting in harm to our health. It simply does not work to treat emotion as an inconvenience, as an adversary, to be controlled or avoided. What is needed is an attitude of allowing, letting this natural energy be expressed.

We consume a tremendous amount of energy in suppressing or repressing emotion. Perhaps you can recall a time of having to hold back anger or some other strong emotion because it would be disastrous to express your true feelings in the situation, such as when you are applying for a bank loan. You wanted to shout or punch the loan officer, but you controlled yourself. Recall how exhausted you felt afterward.

Now remember a situation in which you were openly angry and expressing yourself. Do you recall the level of energy or excitement you felt at the time? It was probably the most "alive" time of your day. This was because you were allowing a very powerful form of energy to flow through you. Every cell of your body was a little more awake because of that blast of life energy. This includes your white cells.

We need to avoid the mistake of labeling emotions as negative or positive, for they are neither. Emotion is simply raw energy, the energy of life. What we *do* with it determines whether it brings us negative or positive consequences.

We will now consider the primary emotions, all of which need full expression: anger, fear, sadness, joy, and love. While there are other terms we sometimes use to describe our emotions, they can generally trace their roots back to these five basics.

ANGER
Anger is a powerful energy of change. For Linda, it was through embracing her anger that she was able to take the step of leaving an abusive marriage. After that change, she was able to get her healing program on track and give herself the time and care she needed. She called this the turning point in her recovery.

When action is needed, anger is certainly a potent fuel. But it can also be vented effectively through writing it out in a journal, telling someone directly how you feel, or expressing it with the body, as we will see in a later exercise.

Many people erroneously equate anger with hostility and shy away from it, thinking that it is destructive. Anger and hostility are not the same. Anger is a simple energy which can energize actions, constructive *or* destructive. Hostility refers to actions which carry an *intention to harm another.*

If you grew up in an environment where anger was only expressed through hostile acts, this distinction may be harder to see. Still, if you are to have a positive attitude toward emotional expression, you must understand this difference. Only then can you reap the benefits of increased energy and mental clarity that can come from fully expressing your anger.

FEAR

Fear, like anger, needs to be acknowledged and expressed rather than buried. It, too, is a form of life-energy moving through you. By allowing its expression you can free yourself from the tension and depletion it can cause.

Recall a time when you felt fear and tried to contain it. Remember keeping a straight face, while feeling the tension or butterflies in your stomach, and the clenching and holding patterns in your body. Now recall the relief of sharing it with someone else. Talking about your fear is one of the most freeing things you can do. Recall Sharon's experience of reporting her fear to her husband during a panic attack (Chapter 5). Merely putting the feelings into words helps the fear dissipate. Let your fear come alive. Feel it as fully as you can. This may even mean exaggerating it at first, by shaking or shivering, or crying.

Confiding in another, writing in your journal, or having a talk with your inner child are all means of helping fear move through. Once you let it be felt completely, it will pass more easily.

SADNESS

Sadness is a healing form of energy, which helps us recover from loss. It may be loss of a relationship, a physical ability, an opportunity, a prized possession, or a dream. Sadness works much like the energy that knits a wound back together. As the healing process expresses itself, the remnants of the wound, such as any scar tissue, gradually diminish until they are almost undetectable. But we must *allow* the healing process to fully express itself. By scratching, rubbing, or otherwise meddling with the wound, we impede the process.

Likewise, healing from loss means the expression of sadness. As with the other emotions, this may be helped by writing, drawing, or sharing with another. It is like excising a wound.

Perhaps you can recall the relief of giving in to what you might call "a good cry." When we truly allow our sadness to move freely through us, there arises a feeling of lightness, harmony, and balance, even a "sweet" feeling. Some people experience a renewed sense of power and potency when they cry heartily.

The good feelings you feel after crying are the evidence that your body has undergone an energetic transformation. You have released a great deal of tension, and you have allowed the energy to move through you. And as it moves through, it helps restore balance in all your bodily systems, including your hormonal and immune systems.

JOY AND LOVE

When we talk about unexpressed emotions, the focus is usually on anger, fear, and sadness. Little or no attention is given to our withholding joy or its close relative, love. And yet, you can probably recall many instances in which you felt genuine joy or love but felt inhibited about expressing it. Perhaps you can recall being left with a feeling of incompleteness.

Since emotion is the energy of life flowing through us, then to block the expression of our joy or love may be just as harmful as blocking other forms of emotional expression. And, as was discussed in Chapter 4 with the study of the Mother Theresa film, such feelings can have a stimulating effect on the immune system.

Bernie Siegel, M.D., has called love the most powerful chemotherapy of all.[1] It may be that something about the experience of love, or even observing it, tells the healing system that life is worth living, and health is worth fighting for. Giving and receiving love involves a movement or flowing of energy. We have all probably experienced the greater feeling of well-being and heightened energy that comes from both giving and receiving.

The Breath

What do you do a thousand times each hour, twenty-four thousand times each day, and eight million times a year, most of the time without realizing it? You inhale. And you exhale.

Of all the sources of energy we use, oxygen is the one most critical to our life on a moment-to-moment basis. You can live without food for days, but air, only minutes.

I have observed a common pattern of shallow and inadequate breathing in people with CFS. Perhaps it is because the syndrome somehow affects the neurology of the breathing process. Or perhaps there is a "background state" of anxiety which causes people to adapt a characteristic pattern of holding or constriction in their chest and rib cage.

In either case, attention to the breath is of particular value in CFS for several reasons. Breathing directly affects your energy level. Shallow constricted breathing keeps you close to a state of oxygen deprivation, hovering around the "poverty line." So, imagine the potential impact on your energy level with just a 2 percent increase in the volume of each breath.

Your white cells are dependent on oxygen to do their healing work, and your marrow requires it in order to produce new, healthy white cells. Your nervous system depends on your breathing to have the energy to orchestrate the myriad of healing responses needed, including communication with your white cells. Oxygen is also needed to help dissolve and release toxins that have occurred as a result of illness, as well as normal metabolism. Taking deep breaths is also the simplest antidote to anxiety attacks, which deprive the body of oxygen and cause it to panic.

An oxygen-rich environment supports all your healing responses, and actually inhibits viruses. On the other hand, an oxygen-poor environment makes it easier for pathogens, many of which are "anaerobic" (living without oxygen), to thrive.

The Breath-Emotion-Energy Connection

We all learned how to control emotions by contracting and constricting certain muscle groups, such as the jaw, the neck and shoulders, or the chest. Of course, holding our breath is the most effective control and suppressant of all. It is the closest we can come to cutting off the flow of energy through the body. Energy, emotion, and breathing are all reduced together.

On the other hand, to increase any one of these can bring increases in the others. As shown in the illustration below, there is a circular relationship among them. With full, deep breathing, there is a dislodging or releasing of held emotion. And when full emotional expression is happening, invariably it is accompanied by fuller breathing. Finally, both of these conditions are accompanied by increased energy.

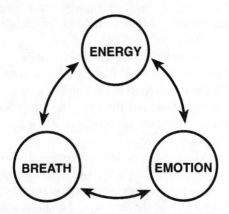

Figure 7. The relationships among breath, emotion, and energy

As a result, if you decide to improve your breathing, be prepared to feel your emotional life more deeply and powerfully. As you increase the availability of energy in your body through breathing, your emotions will come to the surface more readily. For this reason, having a healthful attitude toward emotion and its full expression goes hand in hand with tapping the healing power of the breath.

Full breathing will tend to release pent-up or repressed emotion from the past, which will in turn leave you in a more relaxed state. During a practice session of full breathing, you may find that emotions arise which you had no idea you had. While this may take some getting used to, allowing emotion to flow more freely can only be healing for your body.

Abdominal Breathing

Through conscious awareness of your breathing, and through specific practices, there is a great deal you can do to help your breathing. The most fundamental guideline is to practice abdominal breathing. This means that the point of greatest apparent movement is the abdomen or belly rather than the chest. You might think of the abdomen as a bellows which opens, drawing air in, and then relaxes, pushing the air back out.

Of course, as the abdomen moves and expands, it is really making space for the diaphragm to move and the lower part of the lungs to expand, thereby allowing for more thorough filling and emptying of the lungs. With chest breathing, and without such movement of the abdomen, the lower parts of the lungs are not so free to expand. Breathing will be shallower and less thorough.

Our culture tries to teach us that a tight belly is desirable, and many people try to hold their bellies in and make them stiff like a board. This may fit the current media image of the ideal figure, but it certainly is unnatural, and is counterproductive to healthful breathing. The abdomen should be free to move, with the belly as the point of origin of each breath. Ideally, each breath is like a flowing wave that begins in the abdomen as it expands, followed by the rib cage and chest expanding. On the out-breath, the reverse takes place—the chest and rib cage relax, followed by the relaxation of the belly.

EXERCISE: ABDOMINAL BREATHING

Below is an exercise designed to use gentle breathing movements for breathing more deeply, making more energy available to the body, breathing with less effort, and removing blocks to the breath.

Sit in an upright position with spine erect, or lie flat on the floor, and move gently into *deep, full, relaxed breathing* which after a short while becomes more automatic. Breathe into your belly, letting your belly be the center of your breathing, letting your abdomen expand in all directions, and then let go.

Imagine someone rowing a boat across a pond, and see how their arms move in a continuous, circular motion, with no gap between one stroke and the next. Breathe in this same way, with no separation between breaths. Let each breath flow into the next.

Or picture a tidal pool near the ocean, and see how the water pours in, filling up the tidal pool, and then reverses flow, pouring back out, only to return with the next surge . . . See the continuing, endless process of flowing in and flowing out.

The key is to keep the breath moving. Let your entire torso be involved in the breathing, as if you are opening or expanding all the way from your pelvis to your collarbones. You may even feel a subtle lifting of your collarbones at the top of the breath before letting it all go . . . And as you exhale, gently draw your belly back in, as if you are reaching toward your spine with your navel.

It may help to use your favorite soothing, relaxing music in this process. Let the session last anywhere from fifteen to forty-five minutes, depending on what feels right to you. Some people experience tingling sensations or tightness in parts of the body such as hand, fingers, or lips. This indicates that energy blocks are being opened, and you need not be concerned about this. You also need not be concerned about hyperventilation, which is prevented by maintaining the breathing with *long, slow breaths.* Most of us hypoventilate— that is, we don't take in nearly as much air (energy) as we could use.

As a result of this process, you can become more aware of the potential of your breath in daily life as a source of greater energy, and a device for relaxation and stress reduction.

This can be a very effective and gratifying exercise, especially for people in the midst of an energy crisis. Another benefit is that it can lead to deeper awareness and release of emotions whose presence may not have been fully acknowledged. For some people it can be a highly emotional experience, in which case, professional support may be recommended.

Chi Kung

In 1978 a team of researchers from Harvard Medical School, including Herbert Benson, M.D., visited China to study the mysteries of "chi kung" (also spelled "qi gong"). Every morning at dawn in the parks of Beijing, they witnessed hundreds of people practicing the movements and postures of this five-thousand-year-old tradition.[2]

Chi kung is the mother of all the martial arts. It is estimated that 1.3 *million* residents of Beijing use these practices, with tens of millions more nationwide. In Shanghai there is even a hospital devoted to treating cancer with these methods. Chi kung is the Oriental counterpart of Western behavioral medicine, and contains elements of meditation, relaxation training, visualization, movement, and breathing exercises. In the Orient it serves both as a form of exercise for physical fitness, and a self-healing tool.

In CFS, chi kung can help both with symptoms and with building chi. As Colin, who has had CFS for two years, states, "The chi kung is the one thing I've found that makes me feel balanced again. I used to get a lot of physical pain and nerve inflammation. It calms my body and my nervous system down."

Chi kung offers a good alternative to exercise—which can be beneficial but can trigger relapse if you don't know your boundaries. It, too, is a form of exercise, but rather than challenging your aerobic or muscular fitness, it works directly with your energy, strengthening the body from within.

Chi kung uses breathing and visualization to generate and circulate energy. Some practices can be done sitting or lying down. Some even use sexual energy as a potent healing resource. Rather than thinking of sexual energy as something to be discharged through orgasm, it is circulated through the body to build more chi.[3]

EXERCISE: THE SIX HEALING SOUNDS
There are thousands of variations in how chi kung can be done. Some are specifically intended to promote healing of disease processes. An example of this is "the six healing sounds." While most of the methods of chi kung require instruction from a trained teacher, the six healing sounds are simple enough to give you a taste of chi kung. In my experience, this has proven useful for CFS since

it requires no exertion, and can be done sitting or even lying down.

The intention of the six healing sounds is to help restore balance and harmony in the flow of energy through the body. This is done by breathing fully and making certain sounds, sub-vocally, on the out-breath. The vibrations of these sounds cause a resonance in certain organs where emotions are typically held. By making the sound you help energy flow through the organs, releasing any emotional energy that was stagnating there. This clearing or cleaning of the major organs helps the body as a whole to be in balance as a system of energy. It also helps you find a feeling of emotional well-being.

There are postures you can learn which accompany the sounds. A good resource for developing this practice is the work of Mantak Chia, a chi kung master who lives in the United States and has published several books which are available in popular book stores.[4]

The six healing sounds can be a daily practice in which you set aside a regular time to concentrate on this exercise. Here is an introduction to the method:

It is recommended that you do all six sounds in one sitting. Sit with your spine straight on the edge of a seat. Repeat each sound six, nine, twelve, or twenty-four times. As with all the breathing exercises, let the out-breath be long, thorough, and complete as you make the sound.

1. The lung sound. Place your tongue behind your teeth and with a long slow exhalation make the "SSSSSS" sound (as in "hiss"). As you do this, imagine that your lungs are releasing grief, sadness, or depression. Picture these energies being released through your breath, as if they are a cloud being exhaled from the lungs. As the release takes place, imagine that your lungs are being filled with feelings of courage and righteousness.

After completing the number of breaths, rest silently for a few moments, while imagining that the lungs are continuing to make this sound. Then move on to the next sound.

2. The kidney sound. Form your lips in an "O" and with a long slow exhalation make the sound "WOOOOO" as if you are blowing out a candle. The sound is made with the rush of air, not with your

vocal chords. As you make this sound, imagine that you are exhaling fear, which has gathered in your kidneys. Imagine the fear coming out in a cloud, originating in the kidneys and being released through your mouth. Imagine that the fear is being replaced with a feeling of gentleness in the kidneys.

Rest silently, while imagining that the kidneys are continuing to make this sound.

3. The liver sound. With a long slow exhalation make the sound "SHHHHHH" (as in *"sho*e") and imagine that anger is being released from the liver in the form of a cloud, pouring up from the liver and out through the mouth. As the liver empties of this anger, imagine it is filling with feelings of kindness.

Rest silently, while imagining that the liver is continuing to make this sound.

4. The heart sound. Open your mouth wide and with a long slow exhalation make the "HAWWWWWW" sound (as in *"haw*k"). The sound is made with the rush of air, not the vocal chords. Imagine that any feelings of impatience, hate, or arrogance are being exhaled from the heart. Imagine that as these feelings leave, they are being replaced with feelings of joy, love, and happiness.

Rest silently, while imagining that the heart is continuing to make this sound.

5. The spleen sound. Place your tongue against your palate and with a long slow exhalation make the "WHOOOOO" sound. This is a more "throaty," guttural sound than the kidney sound, and it resonates in your chest. Again, the sound is made with the rush of air, not the vocal chords. As you make this sound, imagine that the cloud of worry and anxiety from the spleen is being exhaled out through your mouth. Imagine the spleen is being filled with feelings of fairness.

Rest silently, while imagining that the spleen is continuing to make this sound.

6. The "triple warmer" sound. The triple warmer is the name given to the three large sections of the torso: the upper section (heart, lungs), the mid section (liver, kidneys, stomach, pancreas, spleen), and the lower section (intestines, bladder, sex organs). This sound is best done lying down. The sound is "HEEEEE" made with the rush of air through your mouth. As you make this sound

with a long, slow out-breath, imagine a huge rolling pin flattening out your body from head to toe. This rolling pin is rebalancing all the energies activated by the other sounds, and helps harmonize the energies of the three large sections.

Now rest, and imagine your entire torso and all your organs being very relaxed and comfortable.

The six healing sounds were originally developed as a practice to be used before bed. They have a calming effect on the neurological system, and can help with the sleep disturbance of CFS.

However, they have an added benefit for people who want to deal more effectively with their emotions. Many have had the experience of becoming emotionally aroused and expressing strong feelings, only to find that they have triggered heightened immune activation and a relapse. The hypersensitivity of the immune system is at the root of this problem. The stress response can be triggered unexpectedly or in circumstances that you would not ordinarily consider stressful.

If this has been the case for you, you no longer need to suppress strong feelings. The six healing sounds are a safe and effective method of emotional release that can help you maintain that state of inner equilibrium you seek.

11

Supporting Your Inner Child

"I knew there was a lot of emotional pain, but I didn't know where it was coming from. I especially worked on allowing my inner child to exist, because I found I had never really been a child. I was always the adult—the 'responsible one'—ever since I could remember."

—Gail

"Spending time with my inner child daily is a top priority. She's become a great friend. I gain energy from talking with her."

—Linda

Throughout this book I have emphasized the importance of lifestyle change and self-help. Yet healthful change is often difficult to maintain. Why do we postpone, or even forget, to follow through with our intentions to help ourselves? In this chapter we will explore one of the most important ingredients in healing CFS: your relationship with yourself.

"Relationship" implies that there are *two*. There are many perspectives on the relationship we have with ourselves. Some people speak of "ego states" relating to each other (Parent, Adult, Child), popularized by the theory of "Transactional Analysis." Others speak of several layers or "levels" of consciousness. Here, we will focus on two aspects of yourself which should be well known to you: what could be called your "wise, mature adult self," and what could be called your "inner child." Symbolically, we use the wise adult self to represent the conscious mind with all its insights, wisdom, and resources. We will use the inner child to represent the subconscious.[1] I find this model of relating to be very helpful in working with our resistance to healthy change.

Consciousness and Change

It has been proven time and again that rational reasons for healthy change are not enough. Research tells us that health education programs often fail because they do not deal adequately with the matter of human motivation. Whether it is public education about smoking, healthy eating habits, preventing sexually transmitted diseases, or any number of other health concerns, the greatest challenge is our resistance to change.

At the heart of this difficulty is the relationship between the conscious and subconscious. While our conscious mind may totally agree with the desirability of a change, our subconscious may have an entirely different opinion. This is usually at the root of noncompliance with healthy behavior change, and it is an obstacle to healing. In an illness like CFS where lifestyle change is paramount, this takes on even greater importance.

Your intention and motivation to change must penetrate more deeply than just your conscious awareness. You must have the cooperation of your subconscious if you hope to change the long-standing habits and preferences to which it has become accustomed. This is because the subconscious is much more vast and powerful than the conscious mind.

The conscious mind can be thought of as the tip of an iceberg, with the subconscious as the vast bulk of the iceberg beneath the surface. Suppose this iceberg is floating along in the Arctic Ocean, and the conscious mind decides it would like to go south for the holidays. The subconscious is used to going north at that time of year, so it says, "What do you mean, south? We always go north. I want to go north." Which way is the iceberg going to go? Who is going to win?

Or think of the subconscious as the automatic pilot in a plane. Suppose you want to fly to Hawaii for the holidays, but the automatic pilot is programmed to always bring your plane to Seattle.

You take off, and before you know it you are stepping down the gangway in your flowered shirt and sandals, only to discover that you're back in Seattle. You forgot to change the automatic pilot.

The subconscious is very slow to change. In fact, it is so committed to its programmed ways of thinking and behaving, that it can easily sabotage your best intentions to change, if these changes go against its programming. The subconscious always prefers the comfortable, the familiar, and the predictable. In a sense, it is addicted to recreating and perpetuating the habits of the past.

Understanding Your Inner Child: Back to Your Roots

The adversity of CFS is felt very deeply. Perhaps the most profound way is in a sense of powerlessness or helplessness. You know something is terribly wrong, and there is no medical cure and little understanding or predictability to it. The result may be feeling out of control of your life, with a gnawing sense of helplessness.

This is not the first time in your life you have felt these feelings. Helplessness, powerlessness, and weakness were a large part of your experience as an infant and small child. The inner child is that part of us which remembers vividly those old feelings of vulnerability. It can be thought of as the simple, innocent, vulnerable part of us which is cohabiting the body of a full-grown, mature, independent adult. But the inner child does not distinguish very clearly the difference between the vulnerability of the past, when you were truly helpless and inadequate, and the vulnerability of the mature adult that you are today. The child believes that, just as when you were physically little, your survival is tenuous today. The experience of chronic illness is extremely distressing for the inner child because it activates those old familiar feelings of helplessness and vulnerability.

In order to develop a healing relationship with yourself, you need to have access to both the inner child and the wise adult self. Ironically, of the two, the most difficult to access is the wise adult self, not the inner child. This is because, contrary to what we may think, it is the inner child who runs our lives 90 percent of the time—and that's on a *good* day. Most of us are totally dominated by the whims, fears, cravings, demands, desires, and strategies of the inner child in our daily living. For many of us, the child dresses up in adult clothes, speaks with an adult voice, and does adult-looking things, but the real force behind these adult actions are the desires, fears, and beliefs of the inner child.

Discovering Your Resources: The Wise Adult Self

The contrast between the full-grown body of the mature adult and the body of a child is an easy one to see. The contrast between your full-grown mind, with its resources and life experience, and your inner child is a little harder to see, but nevertheless, is just as valid.

Your wise adult self knows very clearly the reality that you are not a helpless infant. Even if you are bedridden and debilitated by illness, this helplessness is different from that of a small child. You can still communicate, phone, ask for help, make decisions, and advocate on your own behalf, where a child could not. The adult part of you can see the big picture, the long view, the broader perspective.

The major difference in perspective is that the child gets its identity from the past—memories of helplessness and dependency—while the adult identifies with the present. The child projects the old memories onto the present, and in a sense views the present through very young eyes. The adult self, on the other hand, views the present through the eyes of a full-grown person.

ACCESSING THE WISE ADULT SELF
Even though the inner child may be the dominant force in our lives, we all have the potential of a wise, mature adult within us. We can all describe the qualities and characteristics of such a being. Some of these qualities might include compassion, patience, unconditional acceptance, unconditional love, empathic understanding, permission to be oneself, protection of the child's vulnerability, and strength of resolve.

Even if you do not feel you have much experience knowing this part of yourself, you can describe what it would be like. Perhaps you would draw upon your own experience with parents, grandparents, teachers, other caretakers, friends' parents, or even movies, television, or books. Your ability to create this image within makes it possible for you to find these qualities in yourself and to bring this wise self into the service of your inner child.

Forming a Healing Relationship

The healing of CFS involves restoring balance to our lives, and this requires having a healing partnership between the inner child and the wise adult self. Because the child, like the subconscious, has the ability to sabotage your best intentions if it does not agree with your plans, this relationship is essential to your healing. As Tina tells us, "I'm more supportive of my inner child, I give her a chance to speak up. We're more like friends. I don't betray her so much any more. It's just a better relationship."

Through hypnotherapy, Delores discovered that she was molested as a little girl. She believes this forgotten and buried trauma affected her body and helped set the stage for her vulnerability to an opportunistic illness like CFS. "I have a real wounded little girl in there. I learned fear and guilt, and they are what I feel was blocking my healing."

How can you develop this relationship? There are a variety of ways to approach this. On her own, Tina decided to start using writing as a way of communication with her inner child. "I write with my left hand which seems to represent that childlike part of me. Then I write back with my right hand. It really helps me to let the inner child express herself that way. It gives her a voice that doesn't come out any other way."

There are of course countless ways to access the feelings and voice of the inner child. In the following pages I will describe a process which many people with CFS have found very effective. It involves having a dialogue between the wise adult and the inner child. Communication is the key to all relationships, including that with yourself. This process will create an opportunity for you to communicate in a useful way, and to make a clear distinction between important voices within you. By allowing them to get acquainted with each other, you will make it possible to reach higher levels of self-understanding and self-support.

STEP ONE: SETTING THE SCENE
The dialogue is an intimate and very private conversation. This experience should be treated with respect for its importance, as many people have made profound discoveries through this process.

To prepare the scene, use two chairs facing each other, or two cushions on the floor. You will need to move back and forth between the two seats as you conduct the dialogue. Make sure, as with the other self-healing practices, that you are not disturbed by other people, phones, or other distractions during your dialogue.

STEP TWO: ACCESS THE WISE ADULT SELF
As mentioned above, it can be a challenge to access the wise adult self, especially if you have been in a state of emotional upset or illness. However, in order for the dialogue to work, you must *first* access the adult self.

Some people are helped by sitting quietly and simply stating as sincerely as possible, "I wish to access my adult self now." Take a few moments to calm yourself, sit silently, breathe deeply, and allow a state of calm to descend on you. As the mind clears and you become more relaxed, you will find it easier to feel your integrity, strength, and maturity. A period of meditation is the ideal way to access the wise adult self. If you are following a daily practice of meditation or relaxation processes, this would be the perfect precursor to the dialogue.

STEP THREE: CONDUCT THE DIALOGUE

The invitation
As in any new relationship with a child, especially one in which you hope to win a child's trust, a rapport must be established. To do this, you must have an attitude of unconditional acceptance toward the child. You must create a situation where the child feels that whatever it says will be accepted. There is no place for judgment, analysis, preaching, lecturing, or teaching in this process. It is not a process for the wise adult to impart any knowledge or any other

particular input into the child. Rather, the purpose is to create a *context* where the child feels free and uninhibited in expressing itself.

It is only through this free, uninhibited expression that the child will open up and reveal its deepest feelings and thoughts. Hence, especially in the early going, the role of the adult is primarily to invite the child to speak, to create the environment of nonjudgmental, unconditional acceptance, and to listen.

You might begin by simply inviting the child to share whatever it would like you to know. For instance: "I'd like to get to know you better. I'd like to hear anything you would like me to understand better about you, anything at all that you'd like me to know, about our life." This invitation is short, simple, and nonintrusive. You need not try to make any pledges, promises, or deals. It is simply offering an invitation for the child to open up.

The child speaks

After offering the invitation, switch to the other seat. When you are in the child's seat, it is very important that you alter your posture in such a way that you can feel more childlike. Close your eyes, because the world of the child is the inner world. Hunch your shoulders, drop your head, point your toes together, and take whatever postures help you accentuate the feeling of the child. You may even want to alter your voice.

Sitting in the child seat with your eyes closed, simply look within and share whatever you feel like sharing. There is no need for you to make sense. Anything you have to share is welcome. Any feelings, needs, thoughts, whatever is on your mind is welcome. If you feel like being silent, that too is welcome. Anything at all that you would like the adult to hear is fine.

The adult responds

When the child is at a natural stopping point, then get up and move back to the other seat. In making the transition back into the adult, it is very important that you take your time. Stand up, look around the room through the eyes of the full-grown, mature being that you are. Look at your body, feel its size and strength, slap your thighs, whatever it takes to make a clear transition back into the adult state.

One of the most common difficulties in the process is when people forget to make this clear transition.

Figure 8. Suggested postures for dialogue between the adult and the inner child

Whatever the child has to say must be welcomed. In some cases, the child will simply remain silent in the beginning. If this happens, your response can be something along the lines of: "I appreciate your being willing to sit with me. Thank you for being here with me."

The child may express long-held resentments, and say something like: "It's about time . . . You never listen to me, you never pay any attention to me, and I hate your guts." Again, the response needs to be unconditional acceptance and appreciation of the child for its willingness to express itself to you. In this case, you could thank the child for being here and being willing to share its feelings.

It is vital that you maintain a state of unconditional acceptance. This does not mean you have to agree with what the child says. In fact, your focus is not at all on the content of what is being said. Rather, your focus is on the *process,* the establishing of rapport. In a sense, the words are not nearly as important as the experience the child is having of feeling listened to, perhaps for the first time in its life.

The purpose is not for you to react, or even give anything to the child, *other than this experience of being thoroughly heard.* The expression of emotion is in itself curative. Even if the child moves into catharsis about long-standing hurts, your main response must be nondirective, unconditional acceptance, and support.

It is through this experience of being heard that trust will grow. And the more the child feels it can trust you to respond with acceptance, the more it will open up and share its deeper feelings. Also, as this relationship progresses, the child will gradually allow more and more of your energy to be free for use by the wise adult rather than being bound up in internal conflict. Eventually, as the child and adult become closer, there is a kind of merging or fusion together into a unified being.

The process continues

The dialogue process may involve only a few movements back and forth, or it may involve several. In each case, however, when you move back to the adult seat, always thank the child for sharing. In fact, thank the child profusely, for this will further reinforce the child's sense of being respected and appreciated. You might respond something like this: "Thank you for sharing that with me. I really appreciate your willingness to be here with me and tell me about yourself. Is there anything else you would like me to know?" And then move back to the child again.

When we talk about creating a healing relationship with yourself, what do we really mean? As revealed in this dialogue process, the relationship provides an environment which encourages healing. The healing itself is fostered by the expression of deeply felt feelings, the experience of being heard and respected. It is not a matter of your doing any fancy therapy or other techniques that allows healing to occur. Rather it is this simple experience of expressing the unexpressed and being heard, that is most powerful.

Ending the dialogue

Since the wise adult self is better equipped to be the one who runs our life, it is important to always end the dialogue in the adult position. You may want to finish by thanking the child for its sharing, and for its willingness to be your partner. It is always good to reaffirm your commitment to working on your relationship and being available to the child in the future. Again, be sure you end the process as the adult, so the child is not left in the driver's seat of your life.

SAMPLE DIALOGUE: JOANNE

ADULT: I'd like to get to know you better. I'd like to hear anything you have to share with me.

CHILD: (silence)

ADULT: Thank you for sitting with me. I'm interested in anything you might want me to know. But it's all right if you'd like to be quiet. I appreciate that we can spend this time together.

CHILD: Well, I don't want to talk to you.

ADULT: Thanks for letting me know how you feel. Is there anything else you'd like me to know about our life? I'm interested in you.

CHILD: I don't believe you. You never listen to me. And besides, you always work too much. There's never any time to relax or just feel good. There's always pressure. (Starts crying.)

Note here that the details of what the child says are not so important as the process of allowing and inviting the child to express herself. What she's saying may not even be accurate. Joanne has not worked for two years, yet her child is preoccupied with the trauma of overwork. It is healing for the child to have the opportunity to express this. Joanne's child is releasing a great deal of pain from the past which she has been carrying, perhaps for years.

ADULT (after giving the child all the time she needs to cry): I so appreciate you for letting me know your feelings. Thank you again for being here with me. Is there more you can share with me?

CHILD: I'm scared. I hate being sick all the time. I hate living here. I never get enough rest. I feel all alone. You don't take care of me.

ADULT: I'm glad you are sharing these things with me. Is there more you can tell me?

CHILD: You're not feeding me enough. I'm hungry all the time. It never seems like there's enough food. I need more water, too.

This was Joanne's first effort to establish rapport with her child. Remember, in establishing rapport, the most important thing is to help the child feel safe, accepted, and not judged. This is actually a bonding process. The more the child feels accepted, the more she will express, and the stronger will be the bond between her and Joanne.

If Joanne had responded by confronting or challenging the truth of what the child was saying, the child would have closed down. And if Joanne had responded with "solutions" to the feelings expressed by her child, the child would not have had the opportunity to express all that she did. Also, if Joanne had tried to talk her child out of her feelings, this too would have cut the process short.

The strength in this dialogue is that Joanne remained in the receptive, accepting mode. She did not become a rescuer or a therapist. She did not preach, patronize, argue, or try to change anything about her child's experience. This atmosphere of receptivity will allow trust to grow between Joanne and her child. And as this trust grows, the child will gradually share more and more significant feelings.

The more she does this, the more she will unburden herself, and the lighter Joanne will feel. The child will have the feeling of being acknowledged and included in Joanne's life. It may even make itself more known to Joanne, and as time progresses, Joanne will be more intuitively aware of her child's reactions and needs in daily living.

THE FOCUSED DIALOGUE
AND THE ISSUES OF ILLNESS
So far we have been discussing how to simply establish contact and develop a sense of communication with the inner child. I cannot overemphasize the value of simply listening, rather than feeling you have to solve whatever the child presents. Remember, mere expression of feeling is itself curative. I have seen CFS patients' lives transformed by this simple process.

Your child may not always have clear input for you regarding questions you might ask. And also, you must remember that the child's responses are not to be treated as "the truth." You would not ask your child for guidance on what medicine to take, for example.

The child's responses represent its subjective experience, which in itself is a valuable contribution to understanding yourself better.

Once rapport has been established, however, there may be times when you would like to pursue a particular subject with your child. It can be useful to prepare a list of questions to help you explore how your child feels about a particular issue in your life. This can help you understand more deeply your strong reactions to some things, or your resistance to healthy change.

Below is a list of questions which could be used to explore the issues of illness. You could write down the questions with space between them so you can write the answers. In this process, you would ask the question from the adult position, move to the child position to respond, and then move back to the adult position *before* writing down the response.

How well am I taking care of you?
What do you need more of?
What do you need less of?
How well do you trust me to take care of you?
How well am I feeding you?
What do you need in order to sleep better?
How do you feel about our daily treatment routine?
How do you feel about us meditating together?
Are we getting enough relaxation?
How do you feel about the doctor we are seeing?
How do you feel about the medication we are taking?
What do you feel we need in order to help our healing?
Is there anything else you'd like me to know about you?

Loving Yourself

Your relationship with your inner child can be a healing partnership. To the degree that you can clearly access both sides of this relationship, the wise adult self and the inner child, you can create an environment within your body of harmony and peace. This will have a major impact on your body chemistry and your healing process. Many former CFS patients have pointed to the development of this relationship as the turning point in their recovery.

One point on which psychologists and history's spiritual teachers agree is the importance of loving yourself. While this seems to be an ideal on which all agree, rarely are we presented with a practical way of putting that principle into action. To embrace your inner child, and to have an open, unconditional acceptance as demonstrated in this dialogue process, is in fact the fulfillment of that ideal.

12

Using Your Illness as a Teacher

"I feel that I have discovered and recovered a part of my self that had been lost."   —Blanche

People with CFS often find that the syndrome directly challenges all that their lives have stood for. Many have found that to make it through this existential crisis, they have had to find a way to fit this illness into the overall fabric of a meaningful life. In this chapter we will explore how former patients successfully dealt with this aspect of CFS, and how in many ways their lives were deepened and enriched through this experience.

In his book *Man's Search for Meaning,* psychiatrist Viktor Frankl described how people living in tremendous adversity fared better if they were able to find meaning or purpose in their circumstances.[1] Frankl was talking about prisoners of Nazi concentration camps in World War II. Yet we now know that his observations also apply to the adversity of a chronic or life-threatening illness. There is a growing consensus that patients who maintain a sense of meaning or purpose have better medical outcomes than those who do not.

The invitation I would like to offer you in this final chapter is to see illness as a catalyst for personal growth and expansion. In short, you can use your illness as a teacher. If you do, then it is not just a cruel, random act of nature, and you are not simply a helpless victim. You redefine your passage through this illness as a journey of discovery, and you have resources with which you can confront the challenge and achieve mastery over it. Research in health psychology has shown us that people who take such a "challenge" perspective are hardier and recover more quickly from illness.[2]

How Can Illness Be Beneficial?

Psychologists have long been interested in what they call the secondary gains, or benefits, of illness. There are two ways in which illness can be beneficial. One is when it serves to rescue or remove us from unacceptable or unwanted circumstances. The other is when it brings us unexpected insights or discoveries which enrich our lives and advance our growth.

Usually discussions about this subject focus on the role illness serves in helping the person avoid unwanted circumstances. Consider, for example, the child who creates a stomachache on the morning that he doesn't want to go to school, and the stomachache disappears shortly after Mother gives her permission to stay home.

In this case, the illness was created by the person to manipulate a situation and achieve certain benefits. However, one of the most painful things a person with CFS can hear is the suggestion that they created the illness for some gain. Granted, there are many cases where CFS has forced people to make lifestyle changes that turned out to be very desirable, such as quitting a high stress job or leaving a destructive relationship. Yet this illness is far too complex to be something that can be created for such a purpose.

It is certainly worthwhile to examine whether the illness is bringing relief from some otherwise unacceptable circumstance. If this is the case, then you may not be pursuing your recovery program with full commitment.

Our focus here, however, is on the other kind of benefit—one which, for many patients, has been totally unexpected yet greatly appreciated. CFS has served as a teacher and an opportunity for personal growth. As you have no doubt found, this disease can force you to re-evaluate your values, purposes, and whole way of life. Various people have described this illness as a wake-up call or a two-by-four over the head. Perhaps a more sophisticated term is to call it a "pattern-interrupt." This is a term used by hypnotherapists to describe something that interrupts or changes old, unconscious patterns of living or acting, and makes room for something new and better to happen.

Below is an exercise that you can use to discover what CFS may be able to teach you.

EXERCISE: DIALOGUE WITH ILLNESS

In this exercise you will be having a dialogue not with your inner child, but with your illness. To be more precise, the dialogue is between your wise, adult self, and an inner voice that represents the illness. Set out two chairs or two cushions on the floor. Let one seat represent your wise, adult self while the other represents the illness.

In this process you will be physically moving back and forth between the two seats. You begin with a few minutes of silence to prepare your adult self to be completely focused on the process.

When you feel completely present, begin asking the questions below. Each time you ask a question, you move to the other seat to respond as the illness. It is important to actually move in order for the process to work.

When you ask the questions, do so with an objective, casual attitude. You are simply seeking objective information, much like a journalist might do. This is not a confrontation or a healing process. If you have a disdainful attitude toward the illness, its voice will not be as clear and it will not be as forthcoming with information. Remember, all you want from this is information.

In giving your voice over to the illness, it is important that you take your time to relax, close your eyes, and go inside to find an intuitive sense of what the illness might say. When you respond, try to imagine that you *are* the illness talking. Respond as sincerely and honestly as you can.

Begin with the following questions:

1. What are you here to teach me?
2. How well am I learning what I need to learn from you?
3. How do I make it easy for you to remain with me?
4. What will it take for you to leave?
5. Is there anything else I should know?

Spend as much time as you need on each question until you feel satisfied that you understand the answer. If you need to ask for clarification about a response, physically move back and forth between the two seats so as not to blur the two voices together. And each time an answer comes, be sure to thank the illness for speaking to you and helping you understand it.

Always end the dialogue in the adult seat, thanking the illness for being willing to share its secrets with you.

The answers are coming from your subconscious, which is intimately in touch with events in your body. Use the questions as a point of departure to pursue anything else the illness might be teaching you. This is a device you may use regularly, perhaps each day, to monitor your progress.

The balance of this chapter offers the insights of several former or current patients, in what CFS has taught them about living. Though it may sound hard to believe at first, there is a consensus here: The lessons learned are of such great value that they were well worth the price.

Your Relationship with Yourself

CFS forces you to change your relationship with yourself. One of the most common discoveries is that we can actually pay attention and listen to ourselves much more deeply than ever before. Some experience this as listening to inner guidance. Others describe it as listening to the body, as trusting yourself, or as accepting yourself. Consider Tina's story:

"Getting sick was the best thing that ever happened to me. It was what it took for me to really . . . make major changes. I don't think I would have done it otherwise. My body just had to stop me. I wasn't paying enough attention to my life, my stress, my job, and my unhappiness to do anything about it, until I got so sick that I literally could not do anything and had to stop. After that, everything changed.

"I've learned that I always lose when I don't listen to myself, when I don't trust myself. I just have to do things from my heart or my intuition. Otherwise things just go wrong.

"There were signs all along when I was getting sick and would spend four or five days in bed. But I never trusted myself, I would always push myself. Part of me was telling me that something was wrong, that I had to stop and do something, but I didn't listen."

A similar experience is reported by Christy, who states: "I am actually grateful that I got sick, for what I have learned has been that valuable to me. It taught me to slow down and listen to myself. It also taught me that I will never work for money again, only for something I like to do. Money will come, but my job will never run my life again. I will do things that bring me joy."

A variation on this theme is offered by Debbie, who discovered that trusting herself was paramount in coping with CFS:

"What has helped the most has been knowing that what I really feel and sense is true, that I don't have to doubt myself, that what I feel is true for me I can trust. I trust my own thoughts and perceptions. I don't have to live for someone else, not to please twenty million other people, which never worked. I can live my own life for me.

"The hardest thing in coping with this illness was the self-doubt, doubting myself and what I really feel—feeling sick and having other people telling me that maybe I'm making it up.

"What I have learned is that I am me, I can trust me, and I like myself."

Ginger's work with this lesson includes listening to her body as a source of wisdom. We have discussed earlier how symptoms are actually an intelligent effort to restore balance on the part of the body:

"While the initial lesson was learning patience, what I am learning now is to trust my own instincts, my own reasoning and thoughts and insights. I am learning to trust my body's responses to the environment, to irritants, pollutants. I have learned to trust my gut reactions to things rather than the mental processes."

In all of these cases there was a turning inward, and a receptivity toward what was being heard or felt. The relationship with the self became one of being interested in, and trusting, one's own inner experience of life more than before.

Another aspect of this transformation is the obvious shift in attitudes toward self-care. A high degree of vigilance needs to be developed which involves paying attention to your needs on a moment-to-moment basis. Maintaining your sense of balance or integrity becomes a real priority in daily living.

Mike describes his experience as follows: "I take care of myself much better than I ever used to, as far as what I eat and how much sleep I get. Even though I consider myself well, I still have not increased my office hours. I still take two-hour lunches and a day off during the week. I just figure that there are more important things in life than money—such as my family, my health, and my wife."

For Kris, developing a new attitude toward self-care has also been an important outcome. "I have learned that I can influence my health, and I do so very willingly. In the long term, I can affect positively any illness I have. Begrudgingly, I can say I am grateful this illness came now because I needed to learn these lessons. I've had chances in the past and I haven't acted on them. That's one way I've benefited."

As I discussed in Chapter 11, one challenge with which many patients struggle is their own inner resistance to change. Even though we know what is good for us and what would promote recovery, it is still hard to follow through with changes to old habits. Kris describes what it was like for her: "I've learned to laugh at myself, at how stubborn I am. Because I REALLY AM STUBBORN. And there's a little girl inside me who really doesn't want to change. So we have a good laugh every now and then."

SELF-ACCEPTANCE

Tremendous strides in self-acceptance are very common for people who have been through CFS. The syndrome forces people to acknowledge and accept their vulnerability and their limitations. In the process of doing so, there very often is an overall shift toward greater self-acceptance. As Debbie states, "I feel now that whoever I am and whatever state I am in, I'm okay, I love myself."

Self-acceptance also involves acceptance of aspects of your self that were previously denied or discounted, such as your wants and needs. Debbie had previously taken an attitude of self-denial, self-sacrifice, always putting others' wants and needs before hers. This would happen not only in family life but with friends as well. Her belief now is that "My wants and needs are valid, and I say what they are. I may not always get it right now, but I no longer wait for someone else to give me permission or encouragement to have what I want or need."

REDISCOVERING YOURSELF

Much of the suffering brought by CFS is on the mental or emotional level, as a result of having to cope with the limitations on our ability to *do* things. It stands to reason that to the degree that you define yourself by your *actions,* you will suffer more.

Yet many are learning that as this self-image as a "doer" changes, life goes on. They discover that there are dimensions of life other than external accomplishments. They learn that they are valued by others, and can value themselves, simply for being who they are. Consider for example Gail's perspective:

"The big revelation for me was that I am not what I *do.* I discovered that it didn't matter to my husband whether I could do anything or not. Even though I wasn't doing a thing for anybody, there were still people around that loved me. That was a new awakening for me, and that's really what brought me out of the depression. I felt like I was a big zero, but other people were seeing something in me that I couldn't see.

"I began to think that maybe there was something left, maybe I had something within me that I could give. If people could see something in me deeper than my everyday roles, there must be something there and I needed to look for it."

We are not the roles we take on. We are not our careers. We are not our actions. We are much greater and deeper than those external identities. CFS has forced many people to rediscover who they are, and to become very clear about the fact that they are not what they do.

According to Gail, "I became aware that I had always been the rescuer, taking the responsibility for everyone in the world on my shoulders. And I realized that I cannot survive that way. It became evident to me that I needed to learn new skills, such as how to just be 'simple,' how to be present, how to live in this moment."

DISCOVERING YOUR DEEPER VALUES

Related to the lessons about being versus doing is a more general re-examination of values about living. This, naturally, brings different insights for different people. Bernice offers us the following reflections:

"It's made me more compassionate, more understanding. It's made me slow down and smell the flowers, and get off the rat race and start looking at what's real important in life. I think had I not gotten ill, I wouldn't be spending as much time with my children. I'd be at work, and I wouldn't have learned meditation."

For Kris it was a simple message about living in the moment: "I've learned to pay more attention to the present, and worry less about the past and future."

Debbie reports shifts in several values: "I am now happy, and I don't even think I knew what it was to be happy before . . . I've come to believe that what's most important is the quality of relationships—honesty, truthfulness, communication. I say exactly what I feel and what I want. Some people think I'm selfish, but I'm just being honest."

And Gini reveals a deeper reverence for life: "I've learned to cherish life a lot more than I did before, with a lot less taking for granted. I cherish my husband more too, our intimacy and our everyday life."

DISCOVERING INNER STRENGTH

After recovery, people have often reported a new calmness, greater feeling of inner strength, or new confidence in inner resources. Perhaps these changes come from having plumbed the depths of despair and making the journey back to balance. Linda offers her observation:

"If you survive something like Chronic Fatigue Syndrome and don't commit suicide, you have a greater inner strength than you ever had. It was like a trial by fire. That's what I experienced.

"For me, that inner strength came from seeing that life goes on and I didn't need to do a whole lot to survive. Now that I have the energy to do anything I want, I don't have to do all the mundane things that I thought I had to do."

LOOKING WITHIN:
THE VALUE OF INTROSPECTION

One of the most rewarding experiences for me in leading self-help retreats has been in witnessing tremendous breakthroughs of self-discovery. People who would never have had anything to do with introspection or personal growth become genuinely interested in themselves for the first time. Some who would never have considered meditation discover how nourishing and healing it can be simply to become quiet and look within.

I have seen the discoveries that have been precipitated by CFS truly transform people's lives. For example, consider the results of Gail's search:

"I really went on a treasure hunt of the things that I could do to make my life better. First of all I had to look inside and see what was wrong in the first place. One thing was my 'controlling' nature. I had always thought that I could control other people. I thought that if they failed it was my fault.

"I thought my mother's death was my fault. I thought if I had done something better, she wouldn't have died. If I had taken better care of her . . . Realizing that it wasn't my fault or my responsibility that she died was a major step. She had told me many times that she was ready to go, and I didn't want to hear it. Also, realizing that death is not a failure was a real big one for me."

From Sarah's perspective, a great deal of suppressed emotion was unearthed: "I'm finding out that I have been walking around with a lot of angry and frightened feelings for a long time that I simply haven't dealt with."

This theme is repeated by Bernice, who states: "I'm realizing that the purpose of this disease is for me to go within, learn a lot more about myself, and make some incredible changes in order to survive emotionally. I realize that I came from a very dysfunctional background, that there is a lot of learned fear and guilt that seem to be blocking the natural healing energy within me.

"The lesson boils down to my drowning in negative thinking, self-doubt, self-hatred, and guilt all my life. The illness has forced me to realize it, and that those are the very things that are preventing me from getting well. The healing energy's there—I mean, if I cut my finger it heals. It's there, but I was blocking it."

SPIRITUALITY

Times of adversity inevitably bring people more in touch with the spiritual dimensions of life. One result can be a change in the frequency or quality of prayer, as noted by Mike in Chapter 6. This is supported by Gini, who tells us, "I would say overall my spirituality is more alive. We pray on a daily basis. I get the feeling that I can cope with whatever comes, like there is somebody there who is stronger than I am."

It may also mean a wholesale reappraisal of one's spiritual values and belief system. This was the case for Gail, who says: "I had to really look at my religious side and what I believed in. I found that it didn't work for me anymore. And so I started searching for other things of a spiritual nature. I found that meditation did work for me, going inside to find answers, relaxing, quieting my mind, to find my higher self."

Or it may be of a simpler impact, as described by Debbie: "I am healing myself by getting in touch with my true spirit." In all of these cases, the patients agreed that the illness brought them to a greater recognition of the place of spirituality in their lives.

Lessons in Relating to Others

As reflected in Debbie's comments above, having a more accepting relationship with yourself will affect your relationships with others. I have often heard former patients point to a deeper sense of empathy or compassion for others, learning the meaning of forgiveness, and learning to set boundaries in relationships.

EMPATHY AND COMPASSION

The mystics have taught for thousands of years that suffering is a universal and unavoidable human experience. Yet for many of us in modern times, it takes a chronic illness such as CFS to give an experience of the depths of suffering. This will inevitably lead us to a greater ability to empathize with others who are in deep suffering.

A good example of this is offered by Mike, who states: "In my own profession (physician) I believe everything patients tell me now. I have more empathy. After experiencing CFS, I know what it's like to have a chronic illness, so I think I'm probably much more compassionate than I ever was before, and that has been a real help for me in my work."

For Gini the effect was felt in terms of being accepting and nonjudgmental of others: "I've grown in my acceptance of people. I am more patient, and I'm a much less critical person than I used to be."

FORGIVENESS

Many spiritual traditions have taught that forgiveness is healing for the soul. Yet very often we are unaware of resentments we are carrying, which can create an undercurrent of stressful responses in the body. Most likely you have had your share of abuse at the hands of uninformed or insensitive health-care providers, and it would not be unexpected that some resentment is there. Yet forgiveness can be empowering. It helps us let go of the past. It frees up vital energy that may have been going into festering resentments that will never be resolved.

Bernice offers this observation: "One thing that I'm working on now is forgiveness. I'm having to forgive my husband, my mother, my brother, and all the doctors who for four years told me I needed to go to a psychiatrist. I'm working on that a lot, because I don't need to hold that hate inside."

Various rituals can be used to release resentment. An example is to write down a list of all the resentments you are still carrying from the past, going as far back as you can. Then burn the paper and release the resentments from your life as you see them go up in smoke.

SETTING BOUNDARIES

One of the more crucial changes of lifestyle in the recovery from CFS is in setting boundaries. As we shall see below, this issue is played out in many ways. Several aspects of this are summarized in Bernice's statement that, "I've had to set limits and boundaries. My kids have to know what those boundaries are, my friends have to know that I'm ill and I can't make plans beyond today. I've had to educate the people that are around me about my limitations."

It is an issue that comes up within the home as well as with outside relationships. But perhaps the most difficult place to set new boundaries is with family members, where roles have been established for a long time.

Tina offers us an example which would be a stiff test for most anyone, even without CFS:

"My daughter (age seventeen) was very angry with me for not being able to manage things. Even now, it makes her angry, because when I start getting symptoms I start taking care of myself again, putting myself first again. This always affects other people because they want my energy. My daughter had a tantrum, and I simply chose not to respond.

"A few days later she came to me and we had a beautiful talk because I had stood my ground, and she finally accepted it. Standing my ground was good for her in that she realized that I wouldn't always be there for her. That was difficult for her at first because she had always counted on it. She realizes now that she has to be responsible. The breakthrough is not so much that she has more respect for me as that she realizes she isn't always going to get what she wants from someone else."

We could assume that this step toward emancipation for Tina's daughter would have come sooner or later anyway. Yet it was precipitated by Tina's having to set limits in order to care for herself. It reminds us that people, and perhaps children especially, are often more resilient than we give them credit for.

Another area of boundary-setting is in what I call "toxic" relationships. Debbie found that avoiding such contacts was a necessity for her in maintaining her balance. She states:

"I simply try to avoid anyone who is not an uplift for me. My brother and sister, and my in-laws don't understand or accept CFS. So I just don't relate to them. It's too stressful.

"Also my best friend has marital problems, and I haven't spoken to her for months. It's just too much when she wants to talk about her problems, and that's all she wants to talk about. As much as I love her, and she knows this, I avoid her because she's not good for me to be around now. I tell people why I'm avoiding them, and they accept it." This was a gutsy position for Debbie to take, but like Tina, she chose to stick with her boundaries and communicate honestly about them.

Another perspective is offered by Sarah, who was an activist for several years in the CFS patient advocacy movement. After being heavily involved in the information and referral network, as well as support groups, she reached a point where she had to let it all go in order for her healing to progress.

"For almost two years I didn't want to be involved on any level with anyone who had CFS. I was well and it was upsetting for me to be around them, so I kept myself pretty isolated from it. That was all part of my healing process. I needed some distance from it.

"I've been back working with the CFS people this year, but I'm coming back because I believe it's important to stay active in the movement. It's true that I am sad when I see people so ill, but it doesn't pull on me like it used to. I've got my boundaries now, and I can leave it behind."

For many, the lesson of boundaries is that old patterns of accommodation do not work. As Debbie tells us, "I've learned to say no. Not that I'm a bitch, but I used to be a doormat. Now I can say no when I need to—to my mother and my family members, even my best friends." New ways of relating are needed, based on honest communication about needs, energy levels, and willingness or unwillingness to give to others. Many patients have discovered that they must care for themselves first, even though this goes against their old training to always defer to others.

Perhaps it is good to reflect on this compelling insight about how your body keeps itself alive: Your heart pumps blood to itself first.

Couplehood

The effects of CFS on couples have ranged from devastation to transformation. Some relationships do not survive intact, while others seem to flourish. Any couple experiencing a chronic illness undergoes a test of commitment to the relationship. For some the test is an easy one, while others are unable to sustain the stress. For those who do hang in, the rewards are that the relationship is strengthened for having been through the adversity together.

For example, Mike and his wife come from a religious background with a strong family orientation. Through the struggle with CFS, they used some marital counseling to improve their communication skills and ventilate feelings. In retrospect, Mike stated, "I think our relationship is much better than if I hadn't gone through this. It's been a big blessing in disguise."

A similar experience is reported by Gini, who states: "I believe it has strengthened our relationship. He completely revamped his work situation to take care of me, and the result was a lot more intimacy. He now says, 'What I have with you is five hundred times more than I thought I would have in my life.'"

But others had a rockier road before things smoothed out. Gail describes her experience as follows:

"We fought when I was first ill. When I didn't know what was wrong with me, I was angry so I took it out on him. I made his life miserable. I threw him out a couple times. I thought if he can't deal with this, I can't deal with it either.

"I was always angry because I felt I had the responsibility to do everything. Now it's different because I don't feel I have that responsibility.

"Our relationship is now better than it ever was. We communicate a lot more. There's less pushing for things to be done. My husband has learned a lot of patience. The illness helped me to see him differently, too. When I found that I didn't have to be the 'doer' all the time, and I allowed him to do things, then I started seeing him in a different light.

"We're a lot closer. He has said our marriage is one hundred percent better than it was before. He learned that he could lose it, and it frightened him. He'd never really thought about that."

ON BEING A SPOUSE

Being the spouse of a person with CFS can have its own lessons, no less valuable. For Dick, Bernice's husband, there was a period of painful soul-searching over several years. "It got me in touch with what helping one another is really all about," he says, "and that made me a lot deeper. I had to turn within to answer a challenge as severe as this. There was no other way. And that deepened our relationship.

"Either I had to accept it and dedicate myself toward solving it, or give up. There are a lot of people who give up. I'll tell you what: I don't blame them. This is the toughest thing I've ever had to deal with, and I don't even have the disease."

Dick summarizes his learning by saying, "It allowed me to deal with the real core issues. I think we're basically here to learn about relationships, and learn about loving one another."

Deidra, Mike's wife, had a similar experience. The most difficult part of CFS for her was handling Mike's personality changes, and especially coping with his paranoia. "I learned the importance of patience, and having the willingness to endure to the end. I learned tolerance.

"My religious faith was very important. I developed a lot of faith that this was temporary, and that I could live through it. It was clear to me that the situation could either tear our relationship apart or strengthen it."

Now that her husband is well (and jogging four or five miles several times a week), she expresses gratitude that their marriage has continued at a deeper level after CFS.

Acceptance of "What Is"

One of the ways that we add to our suffering is in our nonacceptance of what is true now. Our denial of the truth of our circumstances postpones our acceptance of, and our working with, the present. Energy is consumed by our struggle to hold on to the past, which is impossible and prevents us from living fully now.

One consequence of this for many people with CFS is depression. I refer here to the depression that can arise as a result of our appraisal of our circumstances, not as a result of the chemical changes from the disease process. The antidote to this kind of depression is acceptance of what is true now, and letting go of our fixed ideas from the past about how things should be. This is illustrated beautifully by Debbie, who states:

"I don't get depressed anymore. I used to, but I've learned acceptance. I accept that I could be sick the rest of my life, and I have to just appreciate every day, every moment. And I accept that a miracle could happen and I could recover any day."

Another example is offered by Bernice, who comes from a history of high achievement in many areas of her life. "I have had to realize the fact that I cannot do what I was doing before, owning my own business, running, and being an active mother. I'm having to release that and be okay with what is so now, which is very difficult.

"But I have surrendered to the belief that it's my journey, and that I will come out of it a better person. I try not to dwell on the past and who I was then. I just know that I am becoming someone new."

Bernice and Debbie are among the more severe, long-term cases I have known, each lasting several years. They could easily have caved in to despair, seeing that their lives are not going according to their dreams. Yet they have courageously chosen another path.

Using CFS as a teacher gives you the opportunity to make this a time of growth and self-discovery. You may not have chosen this path of learning if given a choice, but you will certainly benefit for the rest of your life from the lessons it brings you, if you are open to them.

Appendix A

The Centers for Disease Control Criteria for a Diagnosis of CFS

In 1988 the following diagnostic criteria were published in an article entitled "Chronic fatigue syndrome: a working case definition," in *Annals of Internal Medicine,* vol. 108, no. 3, pp. 387–9. The sixteen-member team of researchers and epidemiologists were led by Gary Homes, M.D., from the Division of Viral Diseases, Centers for Disease Control, Atlanta. These criteria are currently under a review process to integrate findings of emerging research and will be revised. They remain the official criteria at this time for a diagnosis of CFS.

A case of the chronic fatigue syndrome must fulfill major criteria 1 and 2, and the following minor criteria: 6 or more of the 11 symptom criteria and 2 or more of the 3 physical criteria; or 8 or more of the 11 symptom criteria.

MAJOR CRITERIA

1. New onset of persistent or relapsing, debilitating fatigue or easy fatigability in a person who has no previous history of similar symptoms, that does not resolve with bedrest, and that is severe enough to reduce or impair average daily activity below 50 percent of the patient's premorbid activity level for a period of at least six months.

2. Other clinical conditions that may produce similar symptoms must be excluded by thorough evaluation, based on history, physical examination, and appropriate laboratory findings.

MINOR CRITERIA:

Symptoms Criteria

To fulfill a symptom criterion, a symptom must have begun at or after the time of onset of increased fatigability, and must have persisted or recurred over a period of at least six months (individual symptoms may or may not have occurred simultaneously). Symptoms include:

1. Mild fever—oral temperature between 37.5°C and 38.6°C, if measured by the patient—or chills. (Note: Oral temperatures of greater than 38.6°C are less compatible with chronic fatigue syndrome and should prompt studies for other causes of illness.)
2. Sore throat.
3. Painful lymph nodes in the anterior or posterior cervical or axillary distribution.
4. Unexplained generalized muscle weakness.
5. Muscle discomfort or myalgia.
6. Prolonged (twenty-four hours or greater) generalized fatigue after levels of exercise that would have been easily tolerated in the patient's premorbid state.
7. Generalized headaches (of a type, severity, or pattern that is different from headaches that the patient may have had in the premorbid state.)
8. Migratory arthralgia without joint swelling or redness.
9. Neuropsychologic complaints (one or more of the following: photophobia, transient visual scotomata, forgetfulness, excessive irritability, confusion, difficulty thinking, inability to concentrate, depression).
10. Sleep disturbance (hypersomnia or insomnia).
11. Description of the main symptom complex as initially developing over a few hours to a few days (this is not a true symptom, but may be considered as equivalent to the above symptoms in meeting the requirements of the case definition).

Physical Criteria

Physical criteria must be documented by a physician on at least two occasions, at least one month apart.

1. Low-grade fever—oral temperature between 37.6°C and 38.6°C, or rectal temperature between 37.8° and 38.8°C. (See note under Symptom Criterion 1.)

2. Nonexudative pharyngitis.
3. Palpable or tender anterior or posterior cervical or axillary lymph nodes. (Note: Lymph nodes greater than 2 cm in diameter suggest other causes. Further evaluation is warranted.)

Appendix B
Current Medical Treatments

The following summary of current medical treatments was compiled by the CFIDS Foundation, San Francisco, and Jonathan Rest, M.D., Chairman of the Medical Training Committee. It is reprinted here with their permission. The CFIDS Foundation produces an excellent newsletter entitled *CFIDS Treatment News*. See Appendix D for how to contact the CFIDS Foundation.

This information is provided in order to help you discuss treatment options with your physician.

I. Treatments known to be effective with other disease processes:

Sleep disorder
Treatment of sleep disturbance is key, as all other symptoms will flare up if the quality of sleep is poor.

Clonazepam (Klonopin) 0.25–2.0 mg by mouth every night at bedtime (Warning: has habit forming potential).
Cyclobenzaprine (Flexeril) 10–20 mg at bedtime.
Sedating antidepressants, especially doxepin (Sinequan).
Temazepam (Restoril), oxazepam (Serax), or other sedative hypnotics.

Pain
Pain is an important clinical manifestation of CFIDS; it can be present in the form of myalgia, neuralgia, and/or arthralgia. In some cases it is quite severe.

Nonsteroidal anti-inflammatories (the newer ones may be especially effective).

Flexeril (see above).

Antidepressants, especially doxepin (Sinequan). Also note that antidepressants are often used in conjunction with sedative hypnotics and/or cyclobenzaprine (Flexeril).

Other stronger analgesics as needed, including narcotics.

Lethargy

Non-sedating antidepressants in low dosages, such as fluoxetine (Prozac) if tolerated—start at 5 mg/day.

See "Associated Autoimmune Disease" below.

Headache

Headaches are frequently pressure-like and unusually severe.

Nonsteroidal anti-inflammatories.

Dichloralphenazone (Midrin) 2 tabs by mouth as soon as headache occurs, and one tab by mouth every hour up to 5/24 hours.

Acetazolamide (Diamox).

Headaches may require stronger pain medication as needed.

Allergy

Treatment of nasal symptoms may improve overall symptom picture.

Cromolyn sodium MDI (Nasalcrom) 2–4 times a day.

Steroid nasal spray.

Non-sedating antihistamines and H2 blockers such as ranitidine (Zantac).

Associated Autoimmune Disease

Thyroid hormone supplementation if autoimmune thyroiditis is present (low dose; don't suppress TSH out of normal range).

Depression

Depression is a significant aspect of the overall symptom picture.

Antidepressants are an important treatment modality. Agents should be selected whose actions may enhance either lethargy, sleeping, or pain control. Initial dosages should be 1/4 to 1/2 the usual starting dose.

II. Treatments which may be effective for CFIDS symptom relief but lack adequate controlled trials:

Pain
Coenzyme Q-10 (a mitochondrial coenzyme utilized in ATP production available in health-food stores): 90–120 mg/day.

Cognitive Dysfunction
Clonazepam (Klonopin): 0.25–2.0 mg by mouth at bedtime.
Nicardipine (Cardene): anecdotal success only.

General Therapy
Vitamin therapy utilizing a good multivitamin/mineral supplement containing additional magnesium and zinc, such as Optivites, at 4–6 a day.
High dose vitamin B-12 injections: Up to 3000 mcg twice a week; must be accompanied by multivitamin supplement (see above).
Magnesium: Magnesium sulfate 1 gram (2 ml), IM weekly for 6 weeks.
Antiviral therapy: Acyclovir (Zovirax) can be effective if laboratory tests suggest acute or persistent viral infection; evaluations of other antivirals are pending.
Immunoglobulin has been effective for many PWCs, although in the literature its use remains controversial (*Amer J Med,* 89, Nov. 1990): IM, 2–4 cc/wk based on weight; IV, 5 gm/wk × 6–12 weeks.
Ampligen may be promising. It is an immune-modulating antiviral drug currently in FDA approved double-blind placebo controlled trials, but is not yet available. Treatment involves weekly IV drug dosing.

III. Treatments which are highly controversial:

Some CFIDS clinicians feel that PWCs may have significant enteric pathogens including fungal and parasitic organisms. Treatment may include antiparasitic and antifungal drugs.

Kutapressin (liver extract): Protocol available through Thomas Steinbach, M.D., Memorial City Medical Center, Houston, Texas.

Appendix C

Programs and Tapes with the Author

RETREATS AND SEMINARS

Dr. Collinge conducts group retreats several times each year based on the principles and practices described in this book. Programs take place at various locations in North America and Hawaii. The retreats are usually residential and offer a comprehensive program of meditation, mind/body medicine, nutrition, massage, using nature as a teacher, and exploring the emotional aspects of illness. Participants include people with CFS, cancer, HIV, and other chronic illnesses. Spouses or partners and family members also participate.

Non-residential programs can be arranged upon request. These often take the form of a weekend workshop, and serve to support people in the use of mind/body medicine with chronic illness.

Continuing education programs for health-care providers are also conducted periodically. These are based on a "provider-centered" approach. Care-givers are helped to recognize and care for their own needs, and use their work in this challenging field as an opportunity for personal growth.

TAPES

Recovering from CFS: The Home Self-Empowerment Program. This four-tape set includes key talks and guided experiences used in author's group retreats and seminars for CFS. The set includes:

Tape 1. Side A. *Hope and Recovery in CFS.* Inspirational talk on the recovery process, the multicausal perspective, the phases of CFS, the 50 percent solution, and related topics.

Side B. *Mind/Body Medicine and CFS*. Explains the benefits of mind/body medicine, and how to avoid common misconceptions that lead to frustration or self-blame.

Tape 2. Side A. *Deep Relaxation*. Guided progressive relaxation exercise leading to the relaxation response.

Side B. *Breath, Imagery, and Healing*. Guided imagery of strengthening and harmonizing the immune system. Uses a unique process of breathing techniques with imagery.

Tape 3. Side A. *Understanding Your Immune System*. Talk on how the immune system works. Gives an optimistic perspective for building confidence in recovery.

Side B. *Breathing and Energy in CFS*. Guided exercises using the power of the breath to build energy for healing and symptom relief.

Tape 4. Side A. *Meeting Your Inner Healer*. A guided imagery experience for accessing the reservoir of wisdom and guidance within. Helpful for managing symptoms, as well as charting your overall course toward recovery.

Side B. *Supporting Your Inner Child*. A gentle guided imagery experience helping you to meet, hear, and embrace your inner child.

Cost: $49.95, includes shipping. (US funds only. Foreign orders add $2. California residents add 7½% tax. Visa/Mastercard accepted.)

For information about retreats and seminars, or to request tapes, write to: William Collinge, Ph.D., P.O. Box 2002, Sebastopol, CA 95473, or phone (800)745-1837.

Appendix D

Organizations for Further Support

Chronic Fatigue Immune Dysfunction Syndrome Foundation
965 Mission St., Suite 425
San Francisco, CA 94103
(415) 882-9986, FAX (415) 882-9758
The CFIDS Foundation is a nonprofit organization founded in 1986 by a group of people with CFIDS. Funded by individual contributions, the San Francisco Department of Public Health, and the San Francisco Foundation, the CFIDS Foundation provides comprehensive information packets for people with CFIDS; daily telephone counseling and referral to knowledgeable physicians, support groups, disability lawyers, and other resources; a periodic newsletter with the latest information on treatments being tried throughout the country *(CFIDS Treatment News);* training and materials for health professionals; patient advocacy and public policy development; media coordination; and support for research.

The CFIDS Association, Inc.
P.O. Box 220398
Charlotte, NC 28222-0398
(800) 442-3437, Information Line (900) 988-2343, FAX (704) 365-9755
The CFIDS Association, Inc. encourages and informs PWCs, their physicians, families, and friends and funds research into the mechanisms and treatment of CFIDS. This is a non-profit organization governed by an all-volunteer board of directors comprised of PWCs and professionals. The association publishes the largest CFIDS journal in the nation, *The CFIDS Chronicle,* and other educational materials; provides local referrals to knowledgeable physicians and support groups, and directly funds CFIDS research and advocacy efforts.

National Chronic Fatigue Syndrome Association
3521 Broadway, Suite 222
Kansas City, MO 64111
(816) 931-4777

This all-volunteer organization consists mostly of patients. It provides scientifically accurate information on CFS to the general public and health-care providers. The following publications are available at nominal cost: *General CFS Packet, Patient Information Packet* (86 pages), *Physician Information Packet* (122 pages), *How to Be a Phone Contact, How to Start a Support Group, Bibliography on CFS* (over 300 citations from 1980–present), *Heart of America News* (quarterly newsletter).

National CFIDS Buyers Club
1187 Coast Village Road, #1-280
Santa Barbara, CA 93108
(800) 366-6056, FAX (805) 565-3946

This patient-owned membership organization makes high-quality nutritional supplements available to people with CFS at discount prices. Many of the products have been recommended by leading CFS physicians and researchers. Some of the profits from the club go to support further CFS research. There is no membership fee. Members receive a catalogue of products, and orders can be placed by mail or phone.

The M.E. Association of Canada
246 Queen St., Suite 400
Ottawa, Ontario K1P 5E4, Canada
(613) 563-1565

This charitable organization provides referrals to physicians and support groups in Canada, and keeps a walk-in library of ME/CFS literature in Ottawa. Volunteers provide phone counseling and referral for callers. The Association publishes a monthly newsletter called "The MEssenger" which is distributed in Canada, England, and Australia, containing news about medical treatment, as well as holistic and alternative therapies.

The Nightingale Research Foundation
383 Danforth Ave.
Ottawa, Ontario K2A 0E3, Canada
(613) 728-9643

This organization conducts research and professional and public education programs for the international ME/CFS community. It sponsors the MESH (M.E. Self-Help) Network which serves as an information and referral source for over nine hundred support groups in North America and Europe, and publishes a newsletter for support group leaders.

The Foundation also publishes a quarterly newsletter of new medical information about ME/CFS, and is publisher of the most comprehensive book on medical aspects. Entitled *The Clinical and Scientific Basis of ME/CFS,* this 750-page volume was compiled by Byron Hyde, M.D., Jay Goldstein, M.D., and Paul Levine, M.D., and contains seventy-five chapters contributed by experts from around the world.

Notes

CHAPTER 1

1. Handleman, M. J. Neurological substrates of behavior: Brain mapping and the chronic fatigue patient. Presented at Chronic Fatigue Syndrome and Fibromyalgia: Pathogenesis and Treatment, First International Conference, Los Angeles, February 1990.
2. Sandman, C. Is there a CFS dementia? Presented at Chronic Fatigue Syndrome and Fibromyalgia: Pathogenesis and Treatment, First International Conference, Los Angeles, February 1990.
3. Caligiuri, M., C. Murray, D. Buchwald, et al. Phenotypic and functional deficiency of natural killer cells in patients with chronic fatigue syndrome. *The Journal of Immunology,* November 15, 1987, vol. 139, no. 10, pp. 3306–13.
4. Herberman, R. Abnormalities in immune system in patients with chronic fatigue syndrome. Presented at Chronic Fatigue Syndrome and Fibromyalgia: Pathogenesis and Treatment, First International Conference, Los Angeles, February 1990.
5. Klimas, N. G., F. R. Salvato, R. Morgan, et al. Immunologic abnormalities in chronic fatigue syndrome. *Journal of Clinical Microbiology,* June 1990, vol. 28, no. 6, pp. 1403–10.
6. Holmes, G. P., J. E. Kaplan, N. M. Gantz, et al. Chronic fatigue syndrome: A working case definition. *Annals of Internal Medicine,* March 1988, vol. 108, no. 3, pp. 387–9.
7. CDC CFS Research Group, Centers for Disease Control, Atlanta, Georgia. Chronic Fatigue Syndrome Research at the Centers for Disease Control. *The CFIDS Chronicle Physicians' Forum,* September 1992, pp. 50–52.

8. Goldstein, J. A. Chronic fatigue syndrome. *The Female Patient,* January 1991, vol. 16, pp. 39–50.

9. Engel, G. L. The need for a new medical model: a challenge for biomedicine. *Science,* 1977, no. 196, pp. 129–136.

10. Ablashi, D. V., S. Z. Salahuddin, S. F. Josephs, et al. HBLV (or HHV-6) in human cell lines. *Nature,* 1987, no. 329, p. 207.

11. Salahuddin, S. Z., D. V. Ablashi, P. D. Markham, et al. Isolation of a new virus, HBLV, in patients with lymphoproliferative disorders. *Science,* 1986, no. 234, pp. 596–601.

12. Buchwald, D., P. Cheney, D. Peterson, B. Henry, S. Wormsley, A. Geiger, D. Ablashi, S. Salahuddin, C. Saxinger, R. Biddle, R. Kikinis, F. Jolesz, T. Folks, N. Balachandran, J. Peter, R. Gallo, and A. Komaroff. A chronic illness characterized by fatigue, neurologic and immunologic disorders, and active human herpesvirus type 6 infection. *Annals of Internal Medicine,* January 15, 1992, vol. 116, no. 2, pp. 103–113.

13. DeFreitas, E., B. Hillard, P. Cheney, D. Bell, E. Kiggundu, D. Sankey, Z. Wroblewski, M. Palladino, J. P. Woodward, and H. Koprowski. Retroviral sequences related to human T-lymphotropic virus type II in patients with chronic fatigue immune dysfunction syndrome. *Proceedings of the National Academy of Sciences U.S.A.,* April 1991, vol. 88:2922–2926.

14. Cheney, P. Is CFS caused by a virus? Talk given at the conference on *Chronic Fatigue Syndrome: Current Theory and Treatment,* Bel-Air, California, May 18, 1991.

15. Cowley, G., and M. Hager. A clue to chronic fatigue: a specific virus is linked to a debilitating disease. *Newsweek,* September 30, 1991, p. 66.

16. Martin, J. Spumavirus associated myalgic encephalomyelopathy: research breakthrough in the study of CFIDS. *The CFIDS Chronicle,* Fall 1991, pp. 2–4.

17. DeFrietas, E. Association of an HTLV-II-like virus with CFIDS. *CFIDS Chronicle,* Spring 1991, p. 22.

18. Cheney, P. Is CFS caused by a virus? M. Loveless, M.D., Immunologic activation syndrome and its association with chronic fatigue syndrome. Talks given at the conference *Chronic Fatigue Syndrome: Current Theory and Treatment,* Bel-Air, California, May 18, 1991.

19. Goldstein, J. Limbic Encephalopathy in a dysregulated neuroimmune network; Curt Sandman, Ph.D., How CFS affects memory; M. Loveless, M.D., Immunologic activation syndrome and its association with chronic fatigue syndrome. Talks given at the conference *Chronic Fatigue Syndrome: Current Theory and Treatment,* Bel-Air, California, May 18, 1991.

20. Gene linked to how AIDS progresses. *San Francisco Chronicle,* July 31, 1991, page A4.
21. Grufferman, S. Epidemiologic investigations of two clusters of CFIDS. *The CFIDS Chronicle,* Spring 1991, p. 90.
22. Pachuta, D. M. Living long and living well: the role of the physician's attitude. *Maryland Medical Journal,* February 1990, vol. 32, no. 2, pp. 189–96.
23. Farzadegan, H., M. A. Polis, S. M. Wolinsky et al. Loss of human immunodeficiency virus type 1 (HIV-1) antibodies with evidence of viral infection in asymptomatic homosexual men: A report from the multi-center AIDS cohort study. *Annals of Internal Medicine,* 1988, no. 108, 785–90.
24. CDC CFS Research Group. *The CFIDS Chronicle Physicians' Forum,* September 1992, pp. 50–52.

CHAPTER 2

1. Hyde, B. A report on the NIH consensus conference redefining CFS. Talk given at the conference on *Chronic Fatigue Syndrome: Current Theory and Treatment,* Bel-Air, California, May 18, 1991.
2. Demitrack, M. Quote from comments in the teleconference "Chronic Fatigue Syndrome: Diagnosing the Doubt," CTV World Television, A Health News Production, USC Instructional Television Network, Los Angeles, 1991.
3. Bell, D. *The Disease of a Thousand Names.* Pollard Publications, Lyndonville, New York, 1990.
4. Cardiac symptoms: What do they mean? *CFIDS Treatment News,* Fall 1991, page 3.
5. Goldenberg, D.L. Fibromyalgia and other chronic fatigue syndromes: is there evidence for chronic viral disease? *Seminars in Arthritis and Rheumatism,* vol. 18, no. 2, November 1988, pp. 111–20.

CHAPTER 3

1. Lloyd is also affiliated with the National Cancer Institute, University of New South Wales, Australia. Quote from comments in the teleconference "Chronic Fatigue Syndrome: Diagnosing the Doubt," CTV World Television, A Health News Production, USC Instructional Television Network, Los Angeles, 1991.

2. Quote from comments in the teleconference "Chronic Fatigue Syndrome: Diagnosing the Doubt," CTV World Television, A Health News Production, USC Instructional Television Network, Los Angeles, 1991.

3. Bell, D. *The Disease of a Thousand Names.* Pollard Publications, Lyndonville, New York, 1990.

4. Bell, D. Retroviral sequences in children with CFIDS. *The CFIDS Chronicle,* Spring 1991, pp. 16–18.

5. Jessop, C. Clinical features and possible etiology of CFIDS. *The CFIDS Chronicle,* Spring 1991, pp. 70–73.

6. Bell, D. Retroviral sequences in children with CFIDS. *The CFIDS Chronicle,* Spring 1991, pp. 16–18.

7. Jessop, C. *CFIDS Chronicle,* Spring 1991, p. 80.

CHAPTER 4

1. Caldwell, C., M. Irwin, and J. Lohr. Reduced natural killer cell cytotoxicity in depression but not in schizophrenia. *Biological Psychiatry,* 1991, 30:1131–8.

2. Kiecolt-Glaser, J., L. Fisher, P. Ogrocki, et al. Marital quality, marital disruption, and immune function. *Psychosomatic Medicine,* 1987, 49:13–34.

3. Temoshok, L. Biopsychosocial studies on cutaneous malignant melanoma: psychosocial factors associated with prognostic indicators, progression, psychophysiology and tumor-host response. *Social Science and Medicine,* 1985, vol. 20, pp. 833–40.

4. Temoshok, L., B. Heller, R. Sagebiel, M. Blois, D. Sweet, R. DiClemente, and M. Gold. The relationship of psychosocial factors to prognostic indicators in cutaneous malignant melanoma. *Journal of Psychosomatic Research,* 1985, 2:139–53.

5. Temoshok, L. Can psychosocial intervention improve survival time in cancer? Talk given at the Commonweal Conference, Stanford University Medical School, January 27, 1990.

6. Temoshok, L., and B. Heller. Stress and "type C" versus epidemiological risk factors in melanoma. Paper presented at the 89th Annual Convention of the American Psychological Association, Los Angeles, August 25, 1981.

7. Rosenman, R., M. Friedman, R. Straus, M. Wurm, R. Kositchek, R. Hahn, and N. Werthessen. A predictive study of coronary heart disease. *Journal of the American Medical Association,* 1964, 189:15–26.

8. Kiecolt-Glaser, J., W. Garner, C. Speicher, G. Penn, J. Holliday, and R. Glaser. Psychosocial modifiers of immunocompetence in medical students. *Psychosomatic Medicine,* 1984, 46:7–14.

9. Glaser, R., J. Rice, C. Speicher, J. Stout, J. Kiecolt-Glaser. Stress depresses interferon production concomitant with a decrease in natural killer cell activity. *Behavioral Neuroscience,* 1986, 100(5):675–8.

10. Kiecolt-Glaser, J., R. Glaser, E. Strain, et al. Modulation of cellular immunity in medical students. *Journal of Behavioral Medicine,* 1986, 9:311–20.

11. Kiecolt-Glaser, J., R. Glaser, E. Strain, et al. Modulation of cellular immunity in medical students. *Journal of Behavioral Medicine,* 1986, 9:311–20.

12. Glaser, R., J. Rice, C. Speicher, et al. Stress-related impairments in cellular immunity. *Psychiatry Research,* 1985, 16:233–9.

13. Glaser, R., T. Gotlieb-Stematsky (eds.). *Human Herpesvirus Infections: Clinical Aspects.* New York: Marcel Dekker, Inc., 1982.

14. Kasl, S., A. Evans, and J. Niederman. Psychosocial risk factors in development of infectious mononucleosis. *Psychosomatic Medicine,* 1979, 41:445–66.

15. Luborsky, L., J. Mintz, U. Brightman, and A. Katcher. Herpes simplex and moods, a longitudinal study. *Journal of Psychosomatic Research,* 1976, 20:543–8.

16. Goldmeier, D., A. Johnson. Does psychiatric illness affect the recurrence rate of genital herpes? *British Journal of Venereal Diseases,* 1982, 58:40–3.

17. Tomasi, T. *The Immune System of Secretions.* Englewood Cliffs, New Jersey: Prentice-Hall, 1976.

18. McClelland, D., and C. Kirshnit. The effect of motivational arousal through films on salivary immunoglobulin. *Psychology and Health,* 1988, 2:31–52.

19. Caligiuri, M., C. Murray, D. Buchwald, H. Levine, P. Cheney, D. Peterson, et al. Phenotypic and functional deficiency of natural killer cells in patients with chronic fatigue syndrome. *Journal of Immunology,* 1987, 139:3306–13.

20. Aoki, T., Y. Usada, H. Miyakoshi, K. Tamura, and R. Herberman. Low natural killer syndrome: clinical and immunologic features. *Nat. Immune Cell Growth and Regulation.* 1987, 6:116–28.

21. Klimas, N., F. Salvato, R. Morgan, and M. Fletcher. Immunologic abnormalities in the chronic fatigue syndrome. *Journal of Clinical Microbiology,* 1990, 28:1403–10.

22. Klimas, N. Immunological markers in CFS and the use of Prozac in CFS. *The CFIDS Chronicle,* Spring 1991, pp. 47–50.

23. Levy, J. CIAS: reflections on a hyperactive immune state. *CFIDS Chronicle,* Spring, 1991, pp. 75–79.

24. Klimas, N., M. A. Fletcher, and R. Patarca. Progress reports. *The CFIDS Chronicle,* Fall 1991, pp. 9–10.
25. Levy, ibid.
26. Cheney, P. Interviewed on CNN Newsource's program "CFS: Unraveling the Mystery," November 1, 1991.
27. Levy, ibid.

CHAPTER 5

1. Pennebaker, J., J. Kiecolt-Glaser, and R. Glaser. Disclosure of traumas and immune function: health implications for psychotherapy. *Journal of Consulting and Clinical Psychology,* 1988, vol. 56, no. 2, pp. 239–45. This landmark research is also reported in Dr. Pennebaker's book, *Opening Up: The Healing Power of Confiding in Others* (New York: Avon, 1991).
2. Daniel Peterson, M.D. Personal communication.
3. Daniel Peterson, M.D. Personal communication.

CHAPTER 6

1. Cheney, P. Interview in "Physicians' Forum," *The CFIDS Chronicle,* March 1991, vol. 1, no. 1, pp. 1–17.
2. Pelletier, K. *Mind as Healer, Mind as Slayer* (New York: Delta, 1978).
3. Optimism aids recovery. *Brain/Mind Bulletin,* October 1990, vol. 16, no. 1, p. 1.
4. Ornstein, R. and D. Sobel. *Healthy Pleasures* (New York: Addison-Wesley, 1989).
5. Sobel, D. Healthy pleasures: the health benefits of sensuality, optimism, and altruism. Talk given at the annual conference of the National Institute for the Clinical Application of Behavioral Medicine, Orlando, Florida, December 1991.
6. Larson, D. *Journal of Religion and Health,* 1990, vol. 28, pp. 265–78.
7. Larson, D. *American Journal of Psychiatry,* 1990, vol. 147, pp. 758–60.
8. Religious faith, mental health linked by "hard" data. *New Sense* (formerly *Brain/Mind Bulletin*), vol. 17, no. 5, February 1992, p. 1.
9. Cheney, P. Is CFS caused by a virus? Talk given at the conference on *Chronic Fatigue Syndrome: Current Theory and Treatment,* Bel-Air, California, May 18, 1991.
10. Susser, M. Personal communication.
11. Jessop, C. Interview. *CFIDS Chronicle,* Spring 1991, p. 90.

CHAPTER 7

1. This very useful term is advocated by Michael Lerner, Ph.D., director of the Commonweal Cancer Help Program in Bolinas, California.

2. Cunningham, A. J. The influence of mind on cancer. *Canadian Psychologist,* 1985; 26:13–19.

3. The Cancer Support and Education Center, formerly known as Creighton Health Institute, 275 Elliott Drive, Menlo Park, CA 94025, phone (415) 327-6166.

4. Collinge, W. Psychosocial outcomes of complementary cancer therapy. *Proceedings of the Society of Behavioral Medicine,* Ninth Annual Scientific Sessions, 1988, Boston, pp. 60–61.

5. Collinge, W. HIV and quality of life: outcomes of a psychosocial intervention program. *Tenth Annual Proceedings,* Society of Behavioral Medicine, 1989, San Francisco, p. 41.

6. Fawzy, I. A structured psychiatric intervention for cancer patients: changes over time in methods of coping and affective disturbance and in immunological parameters (abstract). *General Hospital Psychiatry,* 1991, 13:361–2.

7. Spiegel, D., J. R. Bloom, H. C. Kraemer, E. Gottheil. Effects of psychosocial treatment on survival of patients with metastatic breast cancer. *The Lancet* October 14, 1989, pp. 888–91.

8. Benson, H., J. Beary, and M. Carol. The relaxation response. *Psychiatry,* 1974, 37:37–46.

9. Benson, H. *The Relaxation Response* (New York: Avon, 1976).

10. Kiecolt-Glaser, J., R. Glaser, D. Williger, J. Stout, et al. Psychosocial enhancement of immunocompetence in a geriatric population. *Health Psychology,* 1985, vol. 4, pp. 25–41.

11. Kiecolt-Glaser, J., R. Glaser, E. Strain, et al. Modulation of cellular immunity in medical students. *Journal of Behavioral Medicine,* 1986, 9:311–20.

12. Smith, G. R., J. M. McKenzie, D. J. Marmer, and R. W. Steele. Psychologic modulation of the human immune response to varicella zoster. *Archives of Internal Medicine,* 1985, 145:2110–2112.

13. Imagery influences immune cells. *Brain/Mind Bulletin,* October 1991, vol. 17, no. 1, p. 1.

14. Weidenfeld, S., A. O'Leary, A. Bandura, S. Brown, S. Levine, and K. Raska. Impact of perceived self-efficacy in coping with stressors on components of the immune system. *Journal of Personality and Social Psychology,* 1990, vol. 59, no. 5, pp. 1082–94.

15. Gruber, B. L., N. Hall, S. P. Hersh, and P. Dubois (1986). Immune system

and psychologic changes in metastatic cancer patients while using ritualized relaxation and guided imagery: a pilot study. Paper presented at the Annual Meeting of the American Psychological Association, Washington, D.C., August.

16. Gruber, B. L. (1987). Personal communication. Barry Gruber, Ph.D., Medical Illness Counseling Center, 2 Wisconsin Circle, Suite 530, Chevy Chase, MD 20815. Phone (301) 654-3638.

17. Carl Simonton, M.D. Personal communication.

18. Buchholz, W. M. (1990). The Medical Uses of Hope. Monograph, available from William M. Buchholz, M.D., 851 Fremont Ave., #107, Los Altos, CA 94024. Phone (415) 948-3613.

CHAPTER 8

1. Perls, F. *Gestalt Therapy Verbatim* (New York: Bantam, 1970).

CHAPTER 10

1. Siegel, B. *Love, Medicine, and Miracles* (New York: Harper and Row, 1986).

2. Eisenberg, D. *Encounters with Qi: Exploring Chinese Medicine* (New York: W.W. Norton and Company, 1985).

3. See for example *Taoist Secrets of Love: Cultivating Male Sexual Energy* and *Healing Love through the Tao: Cultivating Female Sexual Energy,* by Mantak Chia and Maneewan Chia. Both are published by Healing Tao Books, P.O. Box 1194, Huntington, New York 11743, and available in popular bookstores.

4. For a more detailed description of this and other chi kung methods, see *Transforming Stress into Vitality* or *Chi Nei Tsang: Internal Organs Chi Massage,* both by Mantak Chia and Maneewan Chia. Published by Healing Tao Books, P.O. Box 1194, Huntington, New York 11743.

CHAPTER 11

1. Of the many approaches to the concept of the inner child, the approach which I find most helpful, and which is represented in much of this discussion, was developed by Jeru Kabbal, Director of the APT Institute, San Rafael, California.

CHAPTER 12

1. Frankl, V. *Man's Search for Meaning* (Boston: Beacon Press, 1963).
2. Kobasa, S. C. Hardiness and health: a prospective study. *Journal of Personality and Social Psychology,* 337, 1–11, 1979.

Index